MARKETING YOUR $EWING BUSINESS

"How to Earn a Profit"

by
Barbara Wright Sykes

Collins Publications
Chino Hills, CA 91709

Marketing Your Sewing Business
How To Earn A Profit
by Barbara Wright Sykes

PUBLISHED BY:
Collins Publications
3233 Grand Avenue, Suite N-294
Chino Hills, CA 91709
orders@collinspub.com
www.collinspub.com

Cover Design by: K-2 Graphix
Photographs by: Captured Moments by Tami
Layout and Design: Ann Collins
Select Graphics: Monique Mejan

Edited by: Gail Taylor
          Ann Collins

Library of Congress Cataloging-in-Publication Data

Wright Sykes, Barbara, 1947-
  Marketing Your Sewing Business: How to Earn a Profit / by Barbara
Wright Sykes.-- 1st American pbk. ed.
     p. cm.
Includes bibliographical references and index.
  ISBN 0-9717824-3-1 (pbk.)
1. Clothing trade--Management.
2. Household linens industry--Management.
3. Handicraft industries--Management.
4. Sewing--Economic aspects.
5. New products--Marketing. I. Title.
HD9940.A2W76 2004
687'.068'8--dc21
               LCCN: 2003013789

DEDICATED TO....

The most phenomenal women:

In loving memory to a special angel, my mother, who gave me the gift of life. And whose spirit still lives on because of her outstanding contribution and generosity to others.

I am blessed because Mother carefully crafted a solid foundation from which I gained the strength, wisdom, and passion to pursue my dreams in spite of the obstacles that may lay before me. She taught me the true meaning of spiritual purpose.

They say it takes a village to raise a child. Each person's love, devotion and care has a significant affect on the growth and development of that child. My life has been touched by a person who has all of those qualities and more—Roxanna.

To Mother and Roxie, the body of this work is dedicated to you.

With love...

Barbara

Acknowledgements

A special thanks to my husband, Fletcher whose dedication and support is priceless. To Austin, thank you for all the prayers and encouragement throughout my life. To my daughters Tiffany and Adrienne, I am pleased that my hard work and dedication has encouraged you to go forward and pursue your dreams. To Dietrich and Jamie Mattie Lee, you are Nana's angels, all that I do is for you. To my father, sisters, brother and Vanodis Jackson (Skippy), this one's for you. To Rachel Anderson, my manager, I couldn't ask for more.

Special thanks to...

My editors, I can't say enough about how much I appreciate your efforts. To my chief editor, Gail Taylor, your commitment to seeing all four of these books to press is without words. You have always been there through every trial and tribulation encountered, with the spirit of a true professional and above all a good friend.

Featured Guest: Diana Cavagnaro, Justine Limpus Parish, Pam Damour, Bonnie L. Motts, Saundra Weed, Connie Amaden Crawford, Jeff Grant, France Harder, Fred Bloebaum, Victoria Woodford Hunter, Susan Khalje, Jane Ambrose Button, and Trenia Bell-Will.

Christi Koop, you are the most talented graphic designer in the industry. You make my covers shine. I love working with you and want to thank you for your patience and love.

Tami, my photographer, you have a special way of working with people to make them feel at ease and enjoy the experience. You are truly a pro.

Monique Mejan, my Executive Assistant, you have done an outstanding job in all your hard work and research. We can look back on it now with great pride and smile.

My literary consultant, Zola (Tracy) Gales, I have yet to thank you for the way you embrace my novels, and the consistent interest and encouragement you offer at each step of the way. You never tire and are always excited and supportive, and for that I can never thank you enough. We will see our way to victory!

Mickie, years and tears can only explain the special relationship a true friend can offer. You have stood by my side through thick and thin. It is especially comforting to look back and know that you have a true friend whom you can depend on. You have been my inspiration for some time now and I must tell you how proud I am of you and what you have accomplished—You are the girl!

Dan Poynter, from day one you have offered advice and given me good information to allow me to flourish in an industry that has many ups and downs. Through your knowledge and expertise I found my literary voice and have maintained a natural passion for writing. There has never been a time that I have called upon you and you haven't been there. Dan, you will never know how much I appreciate you.

Linda Coleman-Willis—it is not often you get the opportunity to bond with someone who is sincerely thoughtful and loving. It has been my pleasure having you as a true friend and a solid supporter of my career and my family. We love you and can not express the gratitude we feel.

Alice, you are one of the strongest women; I admire your ability to handle a multitude of tasks and responsibilities and still find time for a good friend. Your strength is a constant inspiration for all women.

Jerrold Curry, although we may not be blood related, you are truly my brother. I have known you for so long and our special friendship can only be expressed simply by saying—Thank You.

Jamie Young at the WAVE 94.7 radio station, since 1997 you have strapped on your boots and rolled up you sleeves and been there for me 24—7. It just gets no better than that. Thank you Jamie for all your support.

Barry and Arlys Hamdani, we share a common bond in our love of writing. I look back fondly on the countless hours we talk and share our work. It has been a literary pleasure.

My students, clients and colleagues, I am encouraged to move forward and commit my life to pursuing valuable information in hopes that it will be a blessing to both your personal and professional lives. It is because of you I take great pride in burning the midnight oil.

True Friendship Missionary Baptist Church: Rev. and Sister Perkins, Sister and Brother Nash, Sister Pollard and all the beautiful members, I just want to say thank you for being there for me and my family over the years—I love you.

All the bookstores, libraries, newspapers, magazines and radio stations, thank you for your belief and support of my work and for having me as a special guest. You have added so much to my career.

Linda Turner Greipentrog, from the beginning you have embraced my work. I can recall our first conversation in 1991, from that moment on you have been there for me. Thank you, Linda and the staff at Sew News Magazine.

Nancy Zieman, you are truly loved for your belief in me and my first book The "Business" Of Sewing. Nancy, you have always been supportive no matter when I have called you—Thank you.

Sandra Betzina: Sandy you and Dan are so special. We have shared much over the years and you have always risen to the occasion with real interest and love for whatever I was doing; that is truly hard to find.

I would like to express my gratitude to the many individuals who shared, contributed, supported and given so unselfishly of themselves—Thank you from the bottom of my heart.

Table of Contents

	Chapters	**Page**
1	The Power Of Marketing	7
2	Identify, Profile and Demand	13
3	Studying The Competition	17
4	Developing Image and Branding	19
	Logos, Slogans	
5	Selecting an Advertising Approach	23
6	Design Elements	29
	Letterhead, Newsletters	
	Brochures, Catalogs	
	Flyers, Portfolio	
7	Announcements and Grand Openings	45
8	Attracting The Customer	47
9	Marketing Model	51
10	Marketing Ideas for Sewing Businesses	59
	Mail Orders, Travel Agents	
	Maternity Stores, Bowling Leagues	
	Real Estate Offices, Furniture Stores	
	TV/Movie Studios, Drama Departments	
	Day Care Centers, Cleaners	
	Organizations and Associations	
	Beauty Salons and Barber Shops	
	Vendors and Affiliates	
	Church, In-Kind Businesses	
	Fashion, Trade and Trunk Shows	
11	Free Marketing Money	63
	Planning	
	Asking for Funding	
12	Direct Mail	65
13	Getting Free Publicity	69
14	Bridal and Special Occasion	71
15	Custom Tailoring	79
16	Baby and Children's Market	83
17	Home Décor	89
18	Designing A Website	95
19	Trade Shows	101
20	Monitoring Your Progress	105

Appendix:

About The Author	107
Do You Sew For Profit	108
Bibliography	110
Resource Guide	111
Index	112
Products	114
Order Form	119

Let's Get Acquainted...

It's exciting to have a community of elite professionals. We are proud of you. By hearing about you, others will be inspired. We enjoy profiling our sewing professionals in the *Sewing For Profit Newsletter*. Please take a few minutes to tell us about you and your business. Feel free to tell us as much or as little as you desire. Send your info by:

1. Mail: Sewing For Profit--Cheron Porte
   c/o Collins Publications
   3233 Grand Ave., Ste. N-294C
   Chino Hills, CA 91709
2. Email your comments directly to Cheron Porte at: **Sewing4Profit@aol.com**
3. You may fill out the form on line, go to: http://collinspub.com/newsSurvey.htm

Questions:
Can we profile you in our newsletter? ☐ Yes ☐ No
Please send: a. your photo b. photo of studio c. business card d. photos of your work
Have you written any book/articles?
Do you have any sewing tips?

Sewing Specialty
List your field of specialty.
How did you learned this field? Classes, Mentor?

Pricing/Business
How do you establish your pricing guidelines?
How do you establish your Business Policies?
Do you charge for fitting? Explain?
Do you charge a consultation, shopping fee? Give details.
Do you charge mileage when you go to a client's home or business?

Advertising, Marketing and Promotions
How do you market and advertise to get clients?
Do you accept: Visa, MasterCard, American Express, Checks
Do you sell your items wholesale? Give details.
Do you offer your service to other professionals as a subcontractor?
Do you hire employees or subcontract out projects?

Sewing Studio -
Tell us about your sewing studio? No matter if it's a closet.
What made you decide on this type of layout and design?

Making a Profit
Do you sell fabric and notions to your customers?
Do you buy in bulk from a wholesaler?
How did you find the wholesaler?
How do you calculate your mark up to sell to customers?
Do you teach sewing? What courses do you teach?
How do you charge for lessons? Do you give group discounts?

Helping Others
We are compiling an online resource guide to help other sewing professionals. Please help us by providing the following: Name, address and phone number of the following in your city: (list as many as you want):

    1. Fabric Store   2. Sewing and Vacuum Dealers   3. School that teaches sewing

THE POWER OF MARKETING

By October Gary Dahl was selling 10,000 Pet Rocks a day. He was an overnight celebrity and even appeared on The Tonight Show. In just a few months, he sold a million rocks at $3.95 each and became a millionaire.

Wouldn't it be great to get paid what you are worth . . . doing something you absolutely love? What better way to accomplish your goal than to have a thriving sewing business. A large part of such an accomplishment comes out of strategically planned marketing campaigns, and now is the perfect time to market your sewing business.

What we will cover

In *Marketing Your Sewing Business* we will learn how to make collateral pieces for marketing, such as business cards, letterhead, flyers, catalogs and brochures. We will put together a portfolio and design a web site for a sewing business. We will also cover trade shows, unusual marketing ideas, image development, slogans, graphics, branding, assessing consumer needs, your goods and services, creating demand, studying competition, how to attract clients, cost-effective marketing strategies, and how to increase your profit margin. We'll take a look at how trends and seasons can be used effectively, how to monitor the progress of your marketing efforts and more.

The Power of Marketing

Marketing can convince people to buy almost anything! Don't believe it? What about a mustard seed in a glass tube for a necklace? Or, a bald baby with no features resembling anything a mother would love, complete with birth certificate? Then there's the ultimate: How about a rock you can call your very own pet? These and many other products have absolutely no appeal until clever marketing convinces us of its value. Case in point—the infamous "Pet Rock."

I have always had a fondness for marketing. Majoring in business, I was interested in marketing; and being a creative person, I could see the value and the fun marketing could engender. Though I'd always been aware of its value, I didn't become truly aware of the power of marketing until I witnessed a phenomenon. The story I'm about to share with you is one I tell my students and clients I consult with. Many are individuals with little confidence in their ability to market. Or, they're disinclined to market because they believe no one will do business with them anyway. After hearing this story they're always inspired and gain more respect for the marketing process.

The subject of this story is an unlikely product; incredibly common. When I first saw it in department stores, I thought, *Who in the world is going to buy this?* Turns out, in filling a new and highly unusual role, this object came to be in great demand. In December 1975, I became the proud owner of a Pet Rock named Peaches. My purchasing decision was based on my desire to research every aspect of this product in an effort to understand the marketing approach of its creator, Mr. Dahl. It paid off because I learned plenty!

According to my marketing professor, it started with a young genius named Gary Dahl, owner of Rock Bottom Productions. Gary lived in California and worked as an advertising executive. One evening in April 1975, he was socializing with some friends when the conversation shifted to pets. Gary's theory on pets was they were messy, behaved badly, and cost too much money! But Gary had what he felt was the ideal pet. Easy and cheap, with a great personality: His pet was a rock.

Gary's friends found this amusing and teased him mercilessly. They started saying that pet rocks could do all sorts of things and the whole conversation was the beginning of a running, tongue-in-cheek joke.

That night something happened to Gary in the exchange of lighthearted banter. As a result, he spent several weeks writing the *Pet Rock Training Manual.* He spoke to such issues as how to have a happy relationship with a "geological pet" and even included instructions on how to make them roll over and play dead. He went so far as to include how to house train a pet rock. He'd make a joke of it by saying you could place it on some old newspapers because it would never know what the paper is for, and therefore wouldn't require any instructions. Gary decided to take this to the limit; he wasn't satisfied until he finally created a "Pet Rock" to go with the manual.

The story has it that Gary was walking along the beach and found a rock, unsatisfied with that particular rock he visited his local store and found a more expensive rock. It was gray, uniform in size, and he purchased it for only one penny. He got a gift box shaped like a pet carrying case, packed the rock in excelsior, included the instruction manual and had a product!

In August of that same year, Gary unveiled his new find at a gift show in San Francisco and later in New York. Immediately Neiman-Marcus ordered five hundred units. Then he was convinced he was onto something. He used his sales from Neiman-Marcus to impress other retail chains to get on board. He sent out news releases that had a picture of him and boxes of his Pet Rocks. *Newsweek* was the first to carry a story about the new sensation. Now he was well on his way. By October Gary Dahl was selling ten thousand Pet Rocks every day. Gary quit his job, started Rock Bottom Productions and, in just a few months, sold a million rocks at $3.95 each. You can do the math. Gary became an instant millionaire. He laughed all the way to the bank.

He was an overnight celebrity and even appeared on *The Tonight Show.* By Christmas, two and a half tons of rocks had been sold and 75% of all the daily newspapers had run Pet Rock stories telling of Gary Dahl's explanation that each rock was individually tested for obedience before being selected and boxed.

If you weren't around, or you didn't get a Pet Rock, you can buy a classic for around $15 to $25 on today's market. Like Barbie dolls, these generally come in their original packaging. In addition, you can buy a Pet Rock music video vintage 1985, or a Pet Rock Pendant (rock on a chain). So when you think of your sewing business and feel no one will do business with you, think about Gary Dahl. Reflect on how he used a marketing campaign to convince society to buy a Pet Rock. Think about the ultimate result: He became an overnight success—a wealthy overnight success! So, I ask you—what's keeping you from developing a successful marketing campaign?

Gary's Strategy

What were Gary's selling features? Was your answer the rock? Well, it wasn't just the rock. In advertising they use the expression, "You must sell the sizzle as well as the steak!" The rock was the steak; the sizzle was:

1. Love: The consumer had something to love.

2. Nurturing: And something to nurture.

3. Cost-effectiveness: All that love and nurturing for only $3.95, and no responsibility!

What was his strategy? He created a fad by using the concept of a manual and special box in the shape of a pet carrier. He used his first sale to Neiman-Marcus as leverage to convince other retail chains there was demand for his product. He wrote a news release to major newspapers to make them aware of the new fad. He understood the psychology behind why people buy. He appealed to those basic needs through his marketing strategy. He used the words that identified their desires for love, nurturing and an inexpensive pet.

Who really *needs* a pet rock? The purchasing decision on the part of many was more of a fad than anything else. Perhaps there was that small segment of the population who really believed they had something to love and, strangely enough, love them back. At any rate, his plan worked. He offered the public what they wanted at that time, and did so with amazing success. When I think about the utilitarian value of a pet rock, it makes me think I can sell almost anything. Do you remember the Slinky, or the Hula Hoop? It stands to reason that someone with a *real product and service*—say, someone in the sewing arena—could penetrate the market and sell to the ultimate consumer.

Did Gary have any competition to be concerned with? Nobody in the world had thought of packaging a pet rock. He was in a league of his own. It is almost along the same lines as the Cabbage Patch dolls. With these, you had the opportunity to have a birth certificate just as if you had given birth to a real baby. In both cases the inventor looked at consumer needs and wants and created goods and services that satisfied the consumer. The only unusual element is the unsuspecting consumer didn't know they needed a pet rock and a bald-headed doll with a birth certificate until the clever inventors used savvy marketing techniques to help them realize there was a need. They used concepts and creative packaging to create a demand for their goods and services. How hard is that? This only makes us respect the power of marketing even more.

Marketing Objectives

Your objective is to garner your share of the market. In order to do so, you must have a thorough understanding of your customers wants, needs and desires; and what goods and services you have to fill them. It's imperative that you create consumer demand for your goods and services. Your goal is to investigate consumers' buying patterns and behaviors. Consistent market analysis and consumer profiling will give you the ability to structure your marketing campaigns where your efforts generate a significant return on your invested time, energy and financial resources.

For example, let's say through your research you have discovered home owners in your community desire custom drapes, bedspreads, pillows, etc., and your goal is to provide these items. Further research has shown there are only two sewing professionals in your area who offer these services. The demand is so great they are literally turning down business. This increased demand would give you approximately one-third market share of a booming community of home owners. With this kind of information you can attract the clients to you.

Where do you start?

It is wise to start to gather important data such as what we talked about in the previous example. The best way is to start by utilizing primary data. Analyze your daily activities and the various individuals you come in contact with. Think of your field of specialty and ask yourself if these individuals would be potential customers. To this end, you may want to consider: Organizations, executives, attorneys, bankers, salons, cleaners, schools, day care centers, etc. Make your own list of people and businesses with the idea that they are all potential customers. Write down how you see your goods and services being of benefit to them, and structure your marketing campaign around that theme. Your job is to uncover the demand and fill it.

You should constantly be asking, *What can I do to encourage customers to do business with me?* Make a list and then target your campaign accordingly. Don't overlook the fact that Christmas may be rapidly approaching and this can be extremely beneficial to your marketing efforts. Look for future seasons and trends directly related to your specific sewing businesses.

A key to your marketing success is to create communications that are consistent. We will be discussing them in detail later. Consider starting with the following:

1. **Business cards.** Get plenty and hand them out at every opportunity. Check out www.vistaprint.com for some great-looking and inexpensive cards.

2. **A web site.** Make sure it's clean and concise so your prospective customers will have no question as to what it is you're selling. Consider hiring a webmaster.

3. **A simple one-page flyer.** Just like your web site, create something that explains clearly what you offer and why someone should buy it from you. What are you selling? Why would customers want to buy it from you? Let your flyer tell them exactly why!

Marketing through Repurposing

Repurposing is a term I dearly love. So many of my consulting clients have benefited from this philosophy of taking a good or service and changing the direction, adding something to the product, or just considering an altogether new approach to using it. (The Pet Rock was an ordinary rock that had been repurposed.) Repurposing in one's field doesn't mean you must abandon your original plan. It just may mean you are adding something new to your service offerings that fit ideally in the industry in which you serve, and at the same time you are maintaining your initial focus.

The point I want to make is, as you read this chapter think about how you can repurpose something in your career or business to bring additional revenue. An idea could be right under your nose.

The original book, *The "Business" Of Sewing* was written in a manner whereby those starting any type of business could use it. Case in point: I appeared at Barnes and Noble for a book signing and was approached by an engineer who had just lost his job. He picked up *The "Business" Of Sewing*, leafed through it, and said: "I can't believe it! This is a great book. It has everything I need to start my own business." He purchased the book and had me autograph it for him. He later wrote telling me how the business plan had helped him open his new business and how helpful the pricing was for him—even though he doesn't sew. His became the endorsement I needed in order to explain to the bookstores how to position my book in their stores. Now most bookstores cross-reference the book so it's in the Business as well as the Sewing section.

In the fall of one of my busiest seasons, I was working with a young female executive on a wardrobe plan. She had selected several nice fashion-forward designs for her suits. When it came time to select buttons, nothing I showed appealed to her. After a while, she looked up in amazement and pointed at me, exclaiming: "That's what I want; it's the exact color—it's perfect! Do you have any buttons like that?" At first I didn't have a clue she was referring to my earrings. Unfortunately, I had no buttons even remotely resembling my earrings. She encouraged me to find them.

I can recall scouring every fabric store I could find. I even took pictures and sent them to my button and trims manufacturers' representatives; nothing even close. After an exhaustive hunt for what seemed like a needle in a haystack, one morning I picked up my earrings and just examined them. I can't tell you why, but something led me to them. Knowing how much my client liked my earrings, I began to entertain the thought of possibly turning them into buttons. Now I had never done this before, but it was certainly worth looking into.

It was a good thing for me the earrings had been a recent purchase; I was able to pick up several pairs to experiment with. I did my homework to learn how to convert them into buttons. I consulted my local cleaner's on how they would hold up during the cleaning process. By the close of that week my client had exactly what she wanted and I had learned how to repurpose earrings. Turning earrings into buttons was so successful in my business, a publisher asked me to write an article in a book entitled *Sewing Authors and Experts*.

I was on a roll with my new find. I marketed my new offering using my client's picture to demonstrate the concept. I was turning earrings into buttons, shoe clips, hair ornaments—you name it. If the client wanted it, I made it. They loved it. I never set out to do this in my business, and had I not been open to the possibility, it never would have materialized.

Because the process was more labor-intensive than covered buttons, I was compensated handsomely. I printed little instructions and made my customers aware of the transformation. Disclosure is critical in any business. Eventually, they started bringing me their earrings to convert for their projects. I later hired a young man in my community to do the conversions for me. There was a local accessory store in a strip mall that had the best earrings. I would buy them in multiples and have them converted and placed on cards, complete with price stickers. My profit margins on the conversions were 75%. At the close of that year I had made an enormous amount of additional revenue from the conversions. I later learned how to purchase earrings and backings in bulk to further increase my margins. I wasn't able to meet the glue quotas for open-to-buy from those manufacturers, so I called the manager of a store that sold various types of glue. I explained that the glue I needed was being used for resale and he allowed me to use my seller's permit, and he gave me a significant discount on the units I purchased from his store. Remember, there's no mountain you can't climb!

Here is another testament to the fact that repurposing makes sense: I worked on a story about a company who found a way to convert plastic bottles into fabric. I met them at The California Mart during the Fall 1 Market Week. I could not believe what I saw. There was actually clothing on display that was made out of plastic soda bottles. Matter of fact, there were coats made from the converted material and you could not tell the difference. This is the classic example of repurposing. The full story is in the back issues of The "Business" Of Sewing Newsletters—Back Issues. (See order form at the back of this book)

When you discover you have an opportunity like the ones in this chapter, market them and you will be surprised what happens.

IDENTIFY, PROFILE AND DEMAND

2

The success and profitability of your business depends on your understanding the consumer and the competition, plus your ability to market and attract customers by creating demand for your goods and services.

Identifying What Goods and Services You Offer

Are you proficient at sewing bridal, children's clothing, tailoring, art-to-wear, or home décor? At this point a thorough analysis of your knowledge, skill level and expertise is needed to identify what you have to offer the consumer to satisfy their wants, needs and desires. Let's take a look at how we go about accomplishing this goal.

The process is quite simple. Take out a sheet of paper and label it Goods and Services. Make two columns, A and B. In the first column list every task and project performed in your field of specialty. Put an asterisk beside the areas you excel in. In the second column list any products or special services you will offer in your business. For instance, will you offer extended hours for those who wish to do business with you after their normal work hours? Will you offer the use of credit cards for convenience? Will you make on-site visits? If you specialize in bridal, do you offer related products? Consider the possibility of retail items you could offer and make an additional profit from. Perhaps you find it advantageous to sell stockings and shoes. Or, maybe you have an arrangement with a printer and you sell invitations. The opportunities for increased revenue streams are endless when you think about it. All of these issues will become extremely valuable when formulating your marketing campaign to create demand for you business. Now that you have completed your list, it's time to profile your customer and match your goods and services to their needs.

Profiling Your Customer

The next step in your marketing plan is to uncover your market segment by identifying your customer. Finding out w*ho is your customer,* should definitely be uppermost in your mind. There is a simple process you can employ to assist you in answering that question. Start by thinking of your daily activities and the various individuals you come in contact with. In our daily comings and goings we meet and do business with a number of people. Some we have formed strong bonds with and others we simply interact with in passing. Nonetheless, there has been some type of connection formed. Those individuals where you have formulated a strong bond may be aware that you have a business as a sewing professional; others may need to be educated with respect to what goods and services you have to offer. In either case you will have to educate both of them about you and your value as a sewing professional. This is how you avoid price resistance and gain the respect your business so richly deserves.

Whom do you come in contact with? Most likely, the categories of people you encounter include attorneys, bankers, clerks, hair stylists, teachers, secretaries, doctors, dentists, associates, parents, your friends, your parents' friends, sales people, and the lists goes on. Look at each category and ask yourself, *Would these individuals need my type of sewing specialty?* Chances are, the answer would be *Yes*. After looking at that particular group or segment of individuals you feel would be your customers, select the ones you would target your marketing and advertising campaign toward. That particular group, individual or segment of the population would now be classified as your prospective customers.

When it comes to marketing, advertising and promotions, the structure and tone of your message would focus on the needs, wants and desires of that group of people. Later we will discuss how to capture their attention with collateral pieces such as flyers, brochures, business cards and other tools. But for now, I just want you to understand that those are the individuals you would target in your marketing campaign. Stop and make your list. Label it "Potential Customers."

Potential Customers

attorneys	bankers	hair stylist	associates	parents
dentists	clerks	manicurist	sales people	family
doctors	secretaries	esthetician	mechanic	friends
Pharmacist	teachers	masseuse	grocer	Neighbors

When Do I Come In Contact With Potential Customers?

Tune Up

Oil Change

PTA Meeting

Pick Up Children

Monthly Refills

During Office Visits

My Physicals

Childrens Physicals

Who Do I See On A Regular Basis?

Manicurist

Hair Sytlist

Our next hurdle would be matching your goods and services—your sewing specialty—to the needs of that particular market segment. To further enhance your marketing research, you might want to develop a questionnaire and spend some time questioning those individuals as to what their needs would be in relationship to your sewing specialty. Find out what types of services they desire, and what exactly they are looking for in a sewing professional. Find out what would make them want to do business with you. This information would help you fine-tune your marketing and advertising campaign.

How can you perfect your craft in an effort to satisfy the needs and wants of the ultimate consumer? Your particular market segment may have special needs and perhaps there aren't many sewing professionals to fill them.

Through your research, if you discover there is a void in your industry, why not be the one to fill it? One sure way to satisfy the needs of your market is to provide a much-needed service. That would set you apart from your competitors and give you the foundation for higher prices. It is important to understand what it is they want and what you must provide to satisfy those needs. You need to build on that process and consistently perfect your offerings, whether it is in terms of actually sewing the project, offering conveniences, or a combination of both. Perhaps some of the individuals would prefer that you offer extended hours. Maybe these people work and they really would like to see you at times more convenient for them. If this does not pose an interference with your family time, ask yourself if you could possibly stretch your hours, or change them altogether, to make it convenient for those customers. That would be an offering of convenience and you would build that up in your promotional pieces. You would be offering the service of extended hours, which would be viewed as a plus by your customers.

The success and profitability of your business is predicated on the clear understanding of the consumer in the marketplace, and where your business stands in relationship to its competition. It also depends on your ability to market and attract customers through creating demand for your goods and services.

Creating Demand

Creating demand for a business happens on many levels. Everything you do as a sewing professional is directly related to your ability to create demand. A lot of novice entrepreneurs fail to get it. Let me explain what I mean: It starts from the look and feel of your marketing materials. They are the foundation for capturing the initial attention of the consumer; your business cards, letterhead, flyers, etc. They can see the investment made on your part in the quality of the pieces presented to them. Your marketing materials demonstrate that you are indeed taking care of business.

There are other subtle issues that should be considered in order to heighten the consumer's desire to do business with you. The fact that you utilize contracts and business policies is a strong testament to your business ethics and sense of professionalism. The image of you and your company is consistent.

Have you given any thought to what your appearance reflects to the consumer when they see you in a business setting? If you are dressed like a professional; their first impression on meeting you will be that you look like someone who is running a business as a business versus a hobby. You have respect for your business and it shows. This image of you and your business is what will build value for your goods and services in the minds of the ultimate consumer.

What about the way you interact with your customers, and the organization, layout and design of your office and studio? You keep all scheduled appointments in a timely manner. Your office and studio are always decent and in order whenever you greet clients. These facets of your business will show the customer you are professional and you take what you do seriously. You may be surprised to learn that these things create demand.

Other factors that create demand will be discussed throughout this text. A detailed explanation of one of my collateral pieces is in "Attracting The Customer."

Collins Publications Reader-Customer Profile

Our readers enjoy business/tax tips, sewing techniques, and product reviews, inspirational short stories from subscribers, sewing professional profiles, fashion forecast, articles on unusual sewing-related businesses, and a list of national upcoming events.

*Data compiled from online subscribers, customer purchases and surveys. Earlier data alerted the company to the growing need for information in home décor. They started focusing on that segment by offering books, form and online information.

1995	Present
85 % Domestic, and 13 % Foreign	87 % Domestic, and 15 % Foreign
79 % Sew for profit	89 % Sew for profit
11 % Sew for pleasure	21 % Sew for pleasure
20 % Sew Bridal	23 % Sew Bridal
7 % Alterations	12 % Alterations
24 % Custom Sewing	27 % Custom Sewing
17 % Children's Clothing	20 % Children's Clothing
15 % Home Décor	19 % Home Décor
2 % Other Specialty Sewing	7 % Other Specialty Sewing
Embroidery/Knitting (none)	5 % Embroidery/Knitting
Average age range is 25 to 48	Average age range is 22 to 55
65 % are married	71 % are married
73 % are college educated	82 % are college educated
Average income $45,000	Average income $52,000
12 % of our readers are Men	32 % of our readers are Men
28 % also engage in crafts for profit	36 % also engage in crafts for profit

STUDYING THE COMPETITION

You shouldn't study the competition to duplicate their efforts, but to see what you can offer the consumer to make their buying experience with you better.

Is it necessary to study the competition? Absolutely! Remember, as consumer behavior changes, so does the behavior of your competition. For this reason you must keep your finger on the pulse of the marketplace. If you want to survive in business be prepared to devote as much time and effort to understanding your competition as you do your customers. You can bet your clients will study your competition to see whether you are offering the better goods and services. Consequently, if you're unaware of what your competition is doing you cannot compete; you are out of the game before it begins.

How will you conduct a study of your competition? Make it a priority on your list of Things To Do to develop your own research system aimed at studying your competition. Market analysis can be quite involved and somewhat expensive if you hire a professional. For the purpose of the home-based sewing business or a small retail sewing establishment, you may not need to get quite as involved as would a large corporation. However, if you expand your business into a strip mall or large commercial location where competition may be fierce, you will need to employ some—if not all—of the following techniques; or hire a professional marketing consultant. A consultant will study your competition for product offerings, services, and convenience, as well as sales volume and so on. Here's how you can do it yourself:

Scenario: You are going to study a small bridal boutique located in your neighborhood. The owner worked out of her home for years and has been in the present location for two years. Since you are starting your business out of your home and her shop is only five miles away, it is imperative that you understand what she is offering her customers and how she is operating her business. You may make several visits to complete your study. You will use the charts to check off whether you completed a task.

Visit the Business: Visiting the business is called shopping the competition. Your visit should take place over several days and at different times of the day so you can see any patterns that may be present. Build into your budget funds to make a purchase while there. Also, gather any literature and register for their mailing list. Without being too conspicuous, try to determine the frequency of sales during your visits. Upon leaving, immediately jot down your findings before you forget what took place. Later you can compare each day's total sales to see if you recognize any significant pattern. Inquire about pricing if they have no printed materials. Services offered will be very helpful to you so you know what you're up against. This will give you something to think about when structuring your service offerings.

Study the clientele as thoroughly as possible. Some of the research can be performed on visits to the location; other research must be done using ingenuity and creativity. You may go to the library and research demographic data in your community to gain a better understanding of the people who patronize the shopping center. Call the chamber of commerce and ask them for assistance. Call the local radio, newspapers and cable stations in the area and ask for a media kit. They generally have the area broken down into the information listed below, with the exception of specific purchases by that bridal store. But they will no doubt have buying habits of the consumers in areas that may shed some light on their specific purchasing power.

Check with other businesses in the center to see if they will tell you the types of clientele that frequent the establishments. Call hotels, florists, bakers, and any business in your community that services the bride and inquire about their customers. On the list below jot down the items you can study over a period of visits and make a note of the ones that require additional research. Your purchase of merchandise should yield the answer to the types of payment methods the bridal shop offers its customers.

Store personnel should be studied during each visit. Look for obvious conduct that would be pleasing to you as a customer. Notice each time you visit if the same employees are present. Ask as many unsuspicious questions of the sales clerks as you can. Notice what they do while they are not helping a customer. Are they engaging in keeping the store neat?

Store image and décor may be areas in which you cannot directly compete if you work out of your home. However, there are other ways to compete with respect to environment. The layout and design of your office and study can reflect aesthetic value and good taste and make the buying experience one of pleasure for your customers.

You don't study the competition to duplicate their efforts, but to see what you can offer the consumer to make their buying experience with you even better. After you compile all the data from your study it's time to put it to good use. By now you have identified your goods and services, profiled your customer, and have knowledge of how to create demand as well as what you will offer to set you apart from your competition. Now it's time to develop our marketing, advertising and promotions campaigns.

Key Points to Study

Customers	Employees	Store
Age	Grooming	Geographic location
Sex	Product knowledge	Rate internal/external image
Ethnic background	Willingness to service customers General	Décor match merchandise
Educational level	attitude concerning the business	Is store conveniently located
Marital & Family status	Do employees interact well	Is the lighting appropriate
Frequency of Purchase	Do they keep merchandise neat	Does store arouse interest
Type of Customer		Business hours
Purchases:	Services	Study frequency of sales
cash, credit, layaway	Deferred payment plan	Inquire about pricing
	Giveaways	
What you should do:	Coupons and Discounts	
Purchase a product	Free delivery	
Get literature	Multiple purchase savings	
Get on the mailing list	Gift wrapping	

DEVELOPING AN IMAGE AND BRANDING

A good slogan will tell the customer they can depend on you, and your company will deliver quality products and services.

Logos

Logos are an important marketing tool. They are your company's first and lasting impression to the consumer. They develop brand awareness, name recognition and promote visual reference through style, shape and color. Your logo paints a mental image of your company in the mind of public—good, bad or indifferent. It has a lot to do with the presentation of the name, which plays a key role in the success of the business. Building a strong image requires that you totally understand your business and your customer, and your company conveys a message to the public that suggests you do. Customers feel confident and safe doing business with companies they recognize. That feeling is generally built through exposing your company to the consumer through radio, print or television.

Most products we buy can be recognized without ever reading the name. Their logos are so powerful they have given them what we call brand awareness. Take the Nike symbol; we know it's Nike before we read the name. You can take away all text on the ad and just leave the logo and you'll know these products. What are some other companies you can think of? How about the golden arches of McDonalds, The Pillsbury Dough Boy, or the mustache created when you drink a glass of milk? These are all examples of brand awareness.

Some companies create logos using graphical fonts (specially designed letters of the alphabet). An example would be Coca Cola. There is no mistaking Coca Cola. Often companies will design their logos with a combination of specially designed fonts and graphics. Take my publisher for example. Their earlier logo had plain text and a graphic that depicted writing books: The use of the open-faced textbook and the quill pen. When we refer to Collins Publications we often call it "CP." They added their initials for a touch of brand awareness. They later updated their logo.

More often than not, throughout a company's growth, maturation and product life cycle, they will find it necessary to update their image, either through packaging or changing their logo. Wrigley's recently underwent a packaging change for their gums. I happened to be in a store and noticed that Spearmint was different, and so was Juicy Fruit. In 2002, Collins Publications changed their logo. The example of the two logos will show you what I mean. (See next page.)

Collins Publications
3233 Grand Avenue
Suite N-294-C
Chino Hills, CA 91709
909-590-2471

1991 to 2002

Collins Publications
3233 Grand Avenue • Suite N-294 • Chino Hills, CA 91709
www.collinspub.com • Email: collins@collinspub.com
Voice: 909-590-2471 • Fax: 909-628-9330

2002 to Present

They still use the books to represent what they do, however their fonts have more of a graphical feel. I like the new logo much better. It's a fresh look and a more contemporary design. They stayed with their basic color scheme of turquoise green and lavender blue, which remains their signature. Coca Cola's signature colors are red and white and 7-Up is green and red. So color also plays an important part in identifying a company's brand name. Some companies have colors designed especially for them, while other select from a Pantone Color System (see *Design Elements* for more on Pantone). Can a color be a logo? Hum.

These simple, but striking images perfectly symbolize this sewing professional's specialty: Designer Hats. (Courtesy of Diana Cavagnaro)

One of the most important elements for a business is to create an image by designing a logo that is representative of the business. Design a logo for your business that is easily recognizable by its style, shape and colors. There are several ways in which you may go about developing a logo. When designing, keep in mind a few key points:

Where, or on what will the logo be placed? (Store sign, newsletters, t-shirts, pencils/pens, billboards etc.) You need to be sure it's reasonably legible if it must fit into very small spaces (like the side of a pen). Examples and more information of the following topics can be found in *Design Elements.*

Color – Warm colors such as red, orange and yellow generate a warm and/or exciting message. Cool colors such as blue, green and purple tend to convey a more reserved tone.

Font – The kind of font you use can give the look and feel to your company. Fonts express attitudes and come in categories. Do you want to send a playful, fun message about your business through your logo? Use a font with few, if any straight lines or serifs. Select a font with mostly straight lines, with or without serifs if you want to convey a more serious or traditional message about your business.

Graphics – If you are a skilled illustrator, you may come up with definitive images you can implement on your own. You can also choose to outsource, hiring a designer who will consult with you on your intentions and aspirations, and execute a customized design for your business. Clip art can be another useful resource for graphics. However, design experts suggest you manipulate the image(s) enough to where you can reasonably call it your own creation. Clip art programs are widely available on most word processing programs and new images can also be added through purchase of additional disk sets for a nominal fee.

Budget –You need to consider what's in the budget, particularly if you are outsourcing. It should be calculated into the advertising expense total.

Slogans

Another way to develop brand awareness and name recognition is with a catchy slogan. Before we discuss slogans, I must confess. I had the most fun writing about slogans. The research alone was worth the effort. I could not believe the number of famous and award-winning ads. Some of the slogans have been around for some time and we're still saying them. Talk about name recognition and brand awareness; this is a true testament to the fact that a good slogan can be an effective marketing tool and have longevity as well.

A slogan, as you can see, leaves a lasting impression on the minds of the consumer. It instills familiarity, builds confidence, and develops brand awareness and name recognition. Just like the logo, you create your image with a slogan. The slogan should say something about your business or the product, and in some cases both. A good slogan can tell the customer they can depend on your company and you will deliver quality products and services.

Slogans have the ability to stimulate the customer to action. Nike is a prime example. People today are still chanting Nike's slogan—"Just Do It!" And many consumers responded by rushing out and buying a pair of their tennis shoes. Sales soared and the word on the street among the age demographic Nike was targeting was: Nike is the happening thing. You are socially accepted in the clique if you have a pair of Nikes.

When developing your slogan, outline what it is you want to say about your company, its goods and services, and convey your message in a clever slogan. Use your slogan where possible to reinforce your message. Before you know it, others will be chanting your slogan, buying your goods and services, and telling others that they should do the same.

On the next page I have a chart. One half has the slogan filled in and the other half lists the product. Supply the missing answers. Some of these slogans and products may be out of your generation, but for those of us in the baby-boomer generation, we know them so well.

Exercises

Below I have taken company slogans and made sentences out of them. It's amazing the meanings you can get combining them together. See if you can guess the names of the products in each sentence.

Identify the Product in Each Phrase or Sentence

1. Be all that you can be. **1 answer**
2. 501 Blues! When it rains it pours. You deserve a break today. Because you're worth it. Double your pleasure, double your fun. Just do it. We'll leave a light on for you. **7 answers**
3. Where's the beef? It's the Real Thing. **2 answers**
4. The pause that refreshes. Good to the last drop. **2 answers**
5. Snap! Crackle! and Pop! Breakfast of champions. Melts in your mouth, not in your hands. Bet you can't eat just one. **4 answers**
6. The Uncola, never had it never will. 99 and 44/100% Pure. **2 answers**
7. Sometime I feel like a nut, sometime I don't. Have it your way. **2 answers**
8. Look sharp, feel sharp. What smells fresh, stays fresh? A hint of minty freshness. **3 answers**
9. Reach out and touch someone. When you care enough to send the very best. **2 answers**

Answers are on page 120

Can you...

Look at the Slogan and Name the Company

You deserve a break today
Be all that you can be
M'm, M'm good
Double your pleasure, double your fun
It's the Real Thing
Just do it
The pause that refreshes
Good to the last drop
Breakfast of champions
When it rains it pours
Where's the beef?

Write Slogan for each Company or Product

Kellogg's Rice Krispie's 1940s
M&Ms 1954
Burger King 1973
Hallmark 1930s
L'Oreal
Lay's potato chips
Almond Joy
Gain
Scope
Levi's jeans 1984
AT&T 1979

Answers are on page 120

To explore more about slogans and their history visit the sites below:
http://www.adage.com/century/jingles.html   http://www.tvacres.com/adslogans_s.htm

SELECTING AN ADVERTISING APPROACH

Tip

A good advertisement must:
Attract attention
Be interesting
Cause action

5

Why should you advertise?

People need to know about you and your services. (Chances are pretty good they're not telepathic!) Furthermore, you more than likely have some competition. Competition, however, does give you the opportunity to differentiate yourself. Go back to your research data gathered during your study of the competition and think about it for a while. What is it that makes you different? What makes your products and services unique? Can you offer more competitive prices? Have you harnessed the most up-to-date skills in your field? Do you house particularly sophisticated equipment that you take full advantage of? Do you have a unique or particularly appealing style? Are you promoting a collection or sale? Whatever it is, your prospective customers need to know who you are and what your business has to offer.

The way to attract the attention of the prospective customer is through a powerful headline. The headline should offer a benefit, state a fact or evoke an emotional response. If done appropriately it will hold a reader's attention and encourage them to read the offer through the use of clever subheads and interesting design elements. The ultimate test of a good advertisement lies in its ability to move the reader to action. They always say close your ad with a call to action. The action usually creates a sense of urgency to visit your store, call for more information, make a purchase, or set up an appointment. In this chapter we shall discover the approaches available to create a powerful advertising piece. At the end of this chapter are words that you can use for your ad pieces.

The Sizzle

Capture the reader's attention with a promise or a benefit. The burning question in the minds of the buyer is always, *What do I stand to gain?* The benefit might be saving money through markdowns, coupons, discount, etc. This works well for bargain seekers. Another approach would be to use a question or state a fact. In your header you could use a question like the one in the "Why Custom Tailored Clothing" ad. Or you could use a statement of fact: "Get the Fit You Deserve With Custom Tailored Clothing."

Promoting a New Item or Product

Consumers love new things, even if it's something old that is repackaged or repurposed. When using this approach select leader words that convey the feeling of newness. Listed below are words that large ad agencies use quite often.

Finally
Announcing
Introducing
Latest or New
Now or At Last

The Informational

This is where you educate, advise or inform your customer. You are actually offering help, or giving them information on why buying the product will solve their problems. Common leaders are listed here.

How To...
Here's How...
Here's Why...
Everything You
Need to Know...

Institutional or Service

People feel safe with companies that have been around for some time. They also like and want good quality and service from those they patronize. Why not capitalize on these features of your company in your headline? It could very well be your slogan that carries the message you need. Here are a few examples.

> Serving the Los Angeles area since 1991
> Quality service for more than a decade!
> Open 7 days a week—We're there for you when others aren't.

Target a Specific Audience

> Men's formal clothing: "Specializing in fine attire and alterations for men"
> Children's clothing: "Custom Clothing for Children"
> Home Décor: "A Personal Touch for Your Home"

Blending

Many top ad agencies will combine, or blend, several approaches to achieve the desired response on the part of the ultimate consumer. Follow their lead and implement this in your headline as well.

> Headline: "At last you can have custom clothing at an affordable price."
> Subhead: "Take advantage of our Spring offer. Call for more information."

A Call to Action

There are certain headlines that inspire action on the part of the reader. They use action words to tell the reader what to do and they arouse a sense of urgency. They open with words and phrases such as:

Get the Facts
Try...
Choose...

Alternative Approaches

Why not capitalize on testimonials from your satisfied customers? Their approval of your business builds credibility in the eyes of a prospective customer. If you have performance statistics or can use comparison data, by all means take advantage of the opportunity. If you are involved in the community and have an upcoming event, why not publicize it? This also builds institutional value for your business as well as goodwill.

Note: If you have difficulty deciding which headline approach to use, you will be safe with the benefit headline simply because consumers are benefit-driven.

Here are some examples of words and phrases that "sell," grouped into two categories:

Personal Services		**Reputation**
Reliable	Customized	X years in community
Friendly	Economical	Know-how
Professional	Knowledgeable	Free estimates
Responsive	As always, Quality	Brand names
Time saving	Free price estimates	Deliveries & Installations
Fast	Customized or Standard	On time
Dependable	Distinctive	Easy terms
Gracious		Honest pricing

Feel free to use these words as you consider your own advertising productions.

Advertising Costs

A rule of thumb before spending a great deal of time and money on traditional advertisements such as radio, television and so on: You must exhaust all non-traditional methods of marketing, promoting and advertising your business. Placing advertisements into newspapers can be very expensive, and can rob you of needed capital. You will have to measure the return on your investment prior to placing that ad. Have the newspaper send you their media kit. A media kit will explain the type of clientele the paper targets, their readership, and many other pieces of valuable information you should have. Before investing capital into any ad campaign make sure it reaches your potential clientele. If it doesn't reach your potential clientele, you'll be wasting good money on the wrong type of advertisement.

Selecting any type of advertisement campaign should not occur without your determining the cost per thousand people your ad will be exposed to. This is known as the *CPM*. Prior to placing any advertisement—be it newspaper, magazine, television, radio, or direct mail—calculate your CPM. How many clients you would need to recapture your advertising dollars and make a profit is your major concern. If you can generate enough to cover the cost you might consider placing the advertisement. Ask for any promotional or special discounts the company has to offer and check to see if they offer any frequency discounts. These are discounts that are available for placing a number of consecutive advertisements.

Gathering Data for Optimal Reach

Once you've identified the audience you want to target for a particular advertising campaign, you might want to do some further research on your own to find out where new prospects might be. If you've already exhausted a direct mail broker for lists, you can also check with other local advertising groups, community groups, libraries, newspapers, and even current customers for your market research.

Think about where your target customers live, their average income level, when and where they tend to shop. And, if they are current customers, notice any purchasing patterns and apply this knowledge to your advertising strategy.

Also review the potential for your products and services. Think about all the ways they might be utilized by the customer. See "Marketing Through Repurposing."

To more clearly differentiate yourself, study the competition's promotions and advertising methods. Find a niche in the market and then capitalize on it.

Budgeting

If you want to increase your sales volume, consider increasing your advertising expenditures. If you do your advertising conscientiously, paying attention to whom you're targeting as well as successful previous campaigns, chances are you'll reap the benefits with increased sales.

Look at your budget in terms of annual, monthly, and quarterly expenditures. Experts generally agree that you should expect to spend approximately 15 percent on advertising if you are a new business, or you are pushing for increased volume. Five percent should be allocated to maintain your current sales volume. Once you have decided on an approximate amount to be allocated for advertising purposes, you need to then break that number down according to medium (newspaper, direct mail, etc.).

Below are recommended percentages for breaking down your advertising budget.

Local directories and Yellow Pages --10 percent

Direct mail --15 percent

Newspaper ads and radio commercials --70 percent (not always appropriate for small businesses)

Special promotions -- 5 percent

Add to these amounts any cooperative advertising (co-op) moneys available from your suppliers, assuming you will meet their requirements for participation.

What to Budget: Any budget you use should allow some flexibility to meet changing conditions. Most small business owners include the following.

Many retailers also include a number of the following in their budget:		
Local newspapers	Samples	Point-of-purchase materials
Directories	Publicity materials	Sales portfolios
Radio time	Videotapes	Instruction sheets
Newspapers inserts	Catalogs	Clinics/seminars/workshops
Direct mail materials	Photographs and prints	Business cards
Local magazine ads	Consumer's information	Home shows
Shopper guides	Booklets and folders	Telemarketing
Television time	Advertising specialties	Market research
Local magazine ads	(gifts and premiums)	Community good will activities
		Social/business memberships

Giveaways: A number of businesses plan giveaways and promote them through traditional means of advertising. If you plan to have giveaways for promotional consideration be certain to analyze the cost-effectiveness first. How much of your profit margin will be affected by this type of promotional campaign? What will be your return on your investment? These are two key questions you must ask yourself before going forward with this type of promotional campaign.

Remember to keep accurate records. You will need them not only for business and tax purposes, but also to determine which ads, commercials, promotions and other activities are worth repeating.

Stretching Your Ad Dollar:

If you are looking for ways to save money on advertising, consider using repeat ads. This saves on production costs, plus some newspapers give discounts for repeats, depending on the number of repeats. If you've planned a new, simple yet concise ad, it won't hurt to repeat it for a while since you don't know how successful it will be. This is especially applicable if you're new in business, though it also applies if you've been around for a while. Another avenue to consider is co-op advertising. See the chapter "Free Marketing and PR Money."

Finally, consider radio or television spot *packages.* Your local broadcast station may offer special spot rates to be aired at prime and/or drive times. Packages are almost always significantly less expensive than a single spot airing, so consider them as you plan your advertising campaign.

Guide for Planning Your Advertising Timelines

Task	Date Scheduled	In Progress	Date Completed Notes
Review copies of other flyers			
Work on messages			
Consult with someone about ideas for flyer			
Select final message			
Make rough draft of text and layout			
Check: Is message appropriate? Effective?			
Find several graphic designers			
Call to set up interviews			
Finalize writing, have someone else proofread			
Choose a graphic designer			
Drop off job, set up delivery date			
Get mailing list ready, or purchase list if needed			
Call several printers for prices and turn around time			
Choose printer			
Proofread flyer (not you!)			
Check: flyer for image and message clarity			
Flyer camera-ready and dropped off to printer			
Get info on bulk mailing from post office			
Print mailing labels			
Assign task			
Pick up flyers from printer			
Affix mailing labels to flyers			
Make staff memo regarding flyer's information			
Take flyers to the post office			
Set up evaluation dates			
Start planning next flyer			
Customer receives flyer			
Monitor results			
Make any warm follow-up calls			

DESIGN ELEMENTS

Good headlines have two components: They make a factual statement to create awareness, and they suggest a benefit to the customer.

6

Designing Tips

As a sewing entrepreneur, you will need to create marketing pieces such as newsletters, flyers, brochures, letterhead, etc. This can be easily done through the uses of desktop publishing. If you're a novice desktop publisher there are two areas where you can gain the greatest improvement in the finished quality of your marketing pieces. First, you will need to enhance your typesetting knowledge. And second, learn the basics of layout and design. This applies whether or not you will be the one designing your pieces. You want your marketing pieces to be effective in attracting the interest of your customer to motivate them to action, and you must have the necessary knowledge to do so.

Over the years of being in business I've learned a great deal about design. However, I am always eager to increase my knowledge base through extensive reading and research. All the classes taken in college on marketing, advertising and promotions have paid off. But I have invested a significant amount of time studying what has worked and what hasn't; that is where I've benefited the most. What I am about to share with you comes from all of these experiences. I share them in hopes that you too, will benefit.

Studying the magazines, newsletters, brochures, etc., of popular businesses to understand their appeal is a must. Take your cues from industry leaders who have a proven track record of successful advertisements. Practice your techniques by emulating what they do.

If you're new to desktop publishing, there are other ways in which you can learn to use your software as well as develop your skills. I would suggest you select an advertisement, catalog, flyer, brochure or direct mail piece you like. See if you can recreate it; the practice will be invaluable. You will gain the knowledge of the tools available in your desktop publishing program and fine-tune your layout and design skills along the way. Also, read magazines related to desktop publishing. Many software programs come with tips on design. Some companies publish magazines and have web sites to help you design using their products. Their services generally are free if you are a registered user of the software.

Subscribe to the leading design magazines. If you can't afford to subscribe, go to the library. There you will find a number of excellent publications on desktop publishing, each providing tips and how-to articles that will be extremely beneficial. Often you will find layout makeovers. Study them to get ideas. Look for, and review the marketing materials that have been winners of design contests; examine the look and feel of the pieces. Try to determine what makes them winners. Look for style, color, layout and design techniques. Try to select other pieces designed by the same company or person. See if you can recognize a style that is associated with them. And finally, join a support group to help you on your way.

In the following, we will discuss general rules of layout and design. We will become more specific with each element we examine. Keep in mind that design is subjective and open to one's own interpretation. There are arguments for and against elements of any design depending on whom you approach. However, there are industry rules, and as we know from life, certain rules of design have been broken by major design firms and proved to be enormously successful. But, for now, we will speak to the issue of general rules of design. As you grow and develop in your business, you may find that some of the rules need to be bent, so to speak, to appeal to your specific customer. If it works—great!

Design Elements

Headings/Headlines – The leading text that has the arduous task of grabbing the reader's attention immediately and holding it long enough to lead them through the reading process. You may also mix bold words throughout the advertisement to accompany the heading as illustrated in the "Why Custom Tailored Clothing" ad in this text. The space the heading occupies is the most important real estate of your ad piece. It can be in several formats: To inform, educate, announce, advise, or to feature sales or service. Some headlines use slogans to convey the message. A great companion to the headline is the graphic. It helps to support the headline and vice versa. In summary, the headline has to do double duty: capture prospective customer's attention and convey your message.

Subheadings – Help your readers organize the information they're about to receive by including subheadings, where applicable, in larger and/or bolder fonts. They too can support the headline and lead the reader through your message. Often, a reader will only read the headline and subheads to surmise whether or not the message fits their needs. So use them to guide the reader to the close—a call to action.

Borders - Borders around an entire piece are not usually necessary. They tend to take up space that could be devoted to the message or purposeful graphics. Save borders for enclosing or highlighting messages you want to stand out as separate, such as advertisements not relating to the main text. Now for the pros of borders: One designer I worked with used borders effectively to encapsulate the entire ad, which when viewed in its entirety, served to draw the reader into the message. The audience and the style of the piece will dictate the use of borders.

White Space – White space is the empty space on an advertisement piece. White space can be a good thing if it is purposeful. You don't want your piece to be too cluttered or your readers' eyes will dance around and never really find a starting or focal point. On the other hand, you want to maximize your printing dollar by communicating everything you intend so your advertisement remains purposeful and compelling.

Consider an effective billboard advertisement as a rule of thumb if you're going to use a lot of white space: The ones that are most effective will draw the eye precisely to some specific graphic, phrase, icon and/or easily identifiable trademark. By leaving nothing but a the simple graphic or copy, a person can easily pick out the point of the communication piece, and is not left wondering who it's from or what it's trying to say. It's okay to use a lot of white space, but do it intentionally and for a specific effect; not because you don't know what to do with the rest of the space. If you are going to fill a lot of your space with text and images, make sure they make sense, and don't overdo or it will simply be hard to read.

Entry Points – Offering multiple entry points for the reader encourages greater readership. By offering more ways to get involved, you'll increase the number of readers. A good example of an entry point would be the use of a subhead that identifies the topic of entry. Others are: Pull quotes that call out a large block of text in the body which you want to either restate or call attention to. A sidebar serves to introduce a new concept or idea with innovative style. A drop cap is a larger font at the beginning of a sentence. You usually see this in books at the start of a new chapter. They tend to draw the eye to the paragraph or sentence and can be quite effective. And finally, the use of charts can recreate information in another way to make it easier for the reader to comprehend. Charts can also help the reader to quickly draw conclusions regarding their desire to make a purchasing decision or employ your services.

Font Style – If you want to convey a professional, credible image, avoid gimmicky font styles. Besides, traditional fonts are usually easier to read. When can you use fancy fonts? If they lend themselves to the message or audience you are trying to capture. For instance, there are some fonts that appeal to children, while bolder fonts speak to the senses of the male population. You certainly wouldn't use a delicate-script font to gain the attention of the male sportswear buyer. Fonts come in two categories: serif and sans serif.

Font Examples

Style	Serif fonts	Sans serif fonts
Normal	Times New Roman Bookman Old Style Arrus BT	Arial Abadi MT Condensed Light Antique Olive
Bold	**Times New Roman** **Bookman Old Style** Arrus BT	**Arial** Abadi MT Condensed Light **Antique Olive**
Italics	*Times New Roman* *Bookman Old Style* *Arrus BT*	*Arial* *Abadi MT Condensed Light* *Antique Olive*
Bold Italics	***Times New Roman*** ***Bookman Old Style*** *Arrus BT*	***Arial*** *Abadi MT Condensed Light* ***Antique Olive***

Serif fonts are traditionally used for the body copy. To help me remember the differences I think of the serif fonts as having little feet. Sans serif fonts are normally found in headlines and subheads. In ad pieces you typically see them use these techniques. In the example below all fonts in the same point size (12) notice the variations in size.

Typesetting guidelines:

Spacing - Use one space between sentences instead of two. Many of you were probably taught to use two spaces when you started typing, but typesetting has evolved with the introduction of personal computer software and printers. With most contemporary word processors, a newer one-space convention between sentences makes for smoother flow of reading and allows you to fit more into a limited space.

Other typesetting symbols - There are symbols and punctuation marks that true typesetters use. For example: Use appropriate quotation marks ("and"), not straight quotes (" and "). The same rule applies to the uses of the apostrophes, never use the straight ones. Use the real symbols for ®, [TM] and ©. Never use open circles that you fill in for bullet points; this is the correct bullet to use: •.

Typeface – Don't over dramatize your piece with a clutter of different typestyles. Sometimes less is more. Try to limit your selection to no more than two or three styles. If your goal is to emphasize a word by using black, bold, italics, bold italics or all uppercase letters.

Style - Stylizing a word requires that you be consistent throughout the marketing piece. If you're going to use the word marketplace and you elect to style it "MarketPlace," don't change in midstream and decide to use Marketplace or Market Place or Market-Place. Phone numbers are another example, and believe me we have all made this mistake. Should it be 1-800-795-8999 or (800) 795-8999? Whichever you select will depend on the style you desire; the point is to be consistent. In truth, this is the one that causes me the most heartburn. I dread typing numbers and to have to consider putting something extra with them just drives me up the wall.

Printing with Color – There are certain models of color in the printing industry and the terminology should be used when ordering a printing job with a commercial print house.

CMYK – This stands for cyan, magenta, yellow and black. In the acronym the "K" stands for the key color, which is black. These are the four colors known as process colors used in a four-color or full-color print job.

RGB – This is red, green and blue. Computer monitors see color in this format. Often you'll scan an image into your computer in RGB. When you send a job to the printer you should convert it to CMYK.

Halftones - In an ad you might see pictures or drawings in many colors. They're referred to continuous tone because each tone blends or harmonizes with the next. They are really a series of small dots of color in the form of CYMK inks. That's right. Just four colors! It took me a while to grab hold of this concept. As the dots are registered closer together the colors appear darker. Likewise, when they are farther apart the color appears lighter. In the CMYK ink process, when you overlay dots of the four colors, the eyes cannot see the individual colors of dots; meaning you don't see the four separate colors. What our eyes see are continuous tones of a particular color. The dots that are laid down in the form of CMYK ink patterns called halftones.

How do we turn these dots into a picture using four colors? In the printing industry the process of turning a continuous tone image into a pattern of dots is called halftone screening. Start by first scanning in your image or picture; from there it becomes an image made up of dots known as a bitmap. You'll need screening software such as PhotoShop, PageMaker, CorelDraw or Publisher, that will take each dot in the bitmapped image and convert it into a grid of smaller dots that will be placed into the nearest CMYK color reference. What you end up with is four halftone screens for each process color: one cyan, yellow, magenta and black. The printer has four color plates used to lay one color on top of the other on the printing press. Thus, you have what is called a continuous tone image with thousands of colors. It's hard to believe four colors can produce such results.

Spot Color - Spot colors are specific color inks that go beyond those produced by CYMK. For instance, you want a specific gold, metallic or jewel tone color. You would achieve it through a matching process called Pantone. Pantone is a trademark vendor that offers a swatch book for color matching. Each of its colors is assigned a name. You may hear those in the profession refer to it as PMS; that's short for Pantone Matching System (www.pantone.com). According to recent statistics, Pantone offers 1,114 spot colors and 14 base colors. While Pantone leads the pack, there are others from which to choose: TruMatch (www.trumatch.com), and Agfa's color guides (www.agfabooks.com) are also contenders in the process color field.

Note: if you are going to require a special color along with your CYMK color for printing, plan on an extra charge for an additional plate for the printing press. It would be wise, if possible, to have the printer match your selection as closely as possible with the CYMK color system. Another key factor to keep in mind is that what you see on your computer screen is not necessarily the color you will get from your printed ad. Try to have your computer screen calibrated and even then you will not get the true color. It is wise to have a service bureau print out a color sample or color key so you can decide whether the final printed output will meet your expectations. Your local instant printer or copy center may have these services, or ask a printer for references.

Color – Color certainly draws more attention than basic black and white. It makes your design shine and adds impact. Color conveys feelings and can create a mood. While there is theory regarding the meaning of color, each person responds to color in his or her own way. This is especially true of certain cultures, ages, races and genders. Take for example the use of fluorescent colors. These generally appeal to the teenage consumer. Primary colors have been known to stimulate children, while softer pastels are ideal for a more mature female consumer. Drama, boldness and strength can be conveyed with colors such as black, red and a combination of black and gold. It is believed that we all share some basic responses to color: bright and warm colors are stimulating; dark, cooler colors tend to be more calming. If you plan to include color in your advertisement remember these general principles about various colors:

Red tends to elicit an emotion of excitement, passion, and even aggression – It is certainly among the more stimulating colors.

Orange generally sends message of happiness; not quite as light-hearted as yellow, but definitely still a warm color.

Yellow is a bright and upbeat color. It's playful and references the light of the sun, so it sends tones of lightness, simplicity and innocence.

Green is associated with life and nature; with growth and astringency. It's a good color for creativity.

Blue is more reserved, traditional, cool and clear. Blue has a calming affect.

Purple is the color of royalty. It's often considered regal and daring.

Violet is associated with intimacy. Certain shades make you feel peaceful.

Black is sinister, sexy, bold and dangerous.

White is pure, sterile and offers a feeling of space. In design it's a place to rest the eye.

Silver and *Gold* denote wealth, riches, sophistication and prosperity.

Paper – This medium can be an important design element. Paper comes in all types, sizes, textures and colors. Use them in combination with other design elements to create the perfect ad. You could very well start with the paper as inspiration for your design, and then move into selecting graphics, text and other color elements. There are a number of specialty paper companies that offer catalogs and have web sites to assist you. Use their catalogs to get ideas about how to use their papers. They show ads and examples of the use of each paper. Large paper houses have samples as well. Check your local phone book for Kelly or Kirk Paper Company or visit their web sites. In some cities they have wholesale distribution centers where you can visit and get samples on site. Another design element associated with paper is the folding and shaping process. Consult with your printer for ideas and special pricing before you start your design campaign.

Photographs - Studies repeatedly show that newspaper readers look first to photographs (before any other kind of graphic), then large headlines, and finally to smaller print when seeking an article of interest. It would make sense then, when designing any form of advertisement to try to include graphics. They will more likely grab your audience's attention than just about any other visual element (besides a large and compelling headline).

Photographs provide greater credibility. They help your customer identify with something more palpable; something recognizable and familiar. When you offer them a visual to correspond to a written description, it helps pull the piece together, making for a more complete image of your business, product and/or service. It is good to include photographs of actual people using the products.. This helps potential customers understand more precisely the purpose of that which you are offering.

In a world where we are bombarded with information—sometimes to the point of overload—a photo image may be among the remaining viable ways to grab your potential customer's attention. Not only are you more likely to garner attention through the use of a photograph, you will help reinforce the idea of what you're selling into their memory more effectively than text-only material. Think about a memorable historical event in your life, personal or otherwise. Chances are you associate this event with some sort of image. It's the image that helps make the memory just that – memorable.

The key to using photos effectively often lies in their simplicity. Don't fill the visual space with anything that isn't purposeful, be it extra people or extra accessories/items (especially if you aren't selling or promoting them). Keep the image relevant and clear. Keep your intended message predominant in your thoughts as you create, and chances are you'll end up with an effective, marketable image. Once you've created an image that you are satisfied with, double- and triple-check with individuals unfamiliar with your intentions and see what they think you are saying with your photo(s).

Graphics – Act very much the same way as photographs when it comes to supporting the headline and subheads of your ad pieces. Use them wisely.

Brochures and Catalogs: Brochures are an excellent way to market your business. Whereas flyers are typically limited to a few key points or perhaps a single special event, a brochure can really give your business a "face" and substance – it's where you can show off a little. It's your chance to expand on who you are and what you offer. Likewise catalogs do much the same. However, the difference is brochures are thought of in terms of having information in foldout panels, whereas a catalog has its information in pages. You can have an 11 x 17 piece of paper folded to make four panels for a brochure. You can take that same size paper, add an another sheet and fold them both together in half, and you have an 8-page catalog with finished size of 5 ½ x 8 ½ . Of course there are other variations available. Check with your printer or designer for options.

A brochure can fall into one of two categories: It can serve as a teaser where you simply hint at what a customer would find once they contact you, or it can display your products and services in fuller detail. You need to decide ahead of time how you wish the brochure to serve you and your customers. No matter the purpose, the most important information you need to include is contact information. If potential customers don't know how to contact you, you have created your piece in vain. Include the name of your business, name of a contact person where applicable, address, telephone, fax, web site, and e-mail. As a group, this information should go at the end or bottom/back of the brochure since this is where customers are accustomed to looking for such information. Be sure to triple-check this section for accuracy.

Include photographs of your products and services, and wherever possible, make sure they're taken with people using them so prospects will understand how your goods/services are used – this can also save time and space on otherwise overly detailed text explanations.

Fully explain the product or service, particularly if the brochure will serve in a function similar to that of a catalog, but keep the explanation concise for the brochure. Give your potential customers a reason to contact you. Can you offer them some sort of "new customer discount," a coupon, or some other freebie? Make an enticing offer and your prospects will have greater incentive to reach you and draw the reader into the brochure by placing a related graphic on the cover that gives them a general overview and feel for your business. Perhaps it is a picture of your store, or a popular featured item. Or perhaps you want to use a collage of items and services.

How will the brochures reach your customers? Will they be mailed? Left on counters? Handed out in person? If it will be mailed, be sure to leave space for mailing information, the customer address and your return address plus space for postage. You may need to devote an entire outer page for mailing information. Also, keep all information free from datedness, particularly if you plan to keep the brochure in circulation for several months or more. If you have a limited time offer and want to highlight that, simply say "offer good while quantities last" rather than stating a specific date. Therefore your remaining ad is unharmed and chances are it will not be discarded as it would have with a date stamp. You want to get as much mileage out of your advertising campaigns as possible. Remember, people don't always act right away. They may hold on to the ad and refer back to it later. If you have planted a date that has expired, once they return they may toss the remainder of good information, thinking it no longer applies as well.

For a great resource for design, production, discounted postage and delivery of business brochures and other mail pieces, check out www.usps.gov. See more on this in the chapter "Direct Mail."

Flyer in Landscape Orientation (horizontal)

Layout and Design

Putting it all together

Purpose: What is the main purpose of your ad? Are you going to capitalize on a theme?

Headline: Review "Selecting an Advertising Approach" to help you write your headline. There are some examples of leader words for headlines to help you get started. Another good way is to write down all your thoughts. Write and rewrite the same idea in different ways until you find something that appeals to you, then choose the best one. The most popular approach is the reader benefit. If you run into writer's block with respect to your headline, stop and write the body copy first, then the headline.

Body copy: Contains the main text of your message. It's a descriptive explanation supporting your headline. The summary is a call to action guiding the reader to next step to enjoy your product or service.

Illustration: This is a photograph, line art or drawing used to attract readers and reinforce ideas in headline or copy. It should show your product in action where possible.

Company Profile: This includes your logo, store name, complete address, telephone numbers, web address and business hours. Don't forget special symbols such as copyright, trademark, etc.

Layout: Finally, you will arrange all the elements to achieve your goal to generate interest and action. Keep your image in mind and the purpose of the design as you draw your reader into your piece. Start with a rough sketch of the layout, and as you move forward polish your copy and rearrange any graphical elements as needed. Run your spell check, proof your copy and have it proofed by a trusted resource for design errors, correct grammar, punctuation and usage. Last, test your ad before investing in the print cost.

Preparing for Print: Before you print your material, you want to ensure it will turn out on paper the way you intend. There are programs available that collect files, fonts and graphics to check them for print-readiness. One such program is FlightCheck, made for both Windows and Mac operating systems. Such a program may be a worthwhile investment as it will save you precious time and energy as you get your advertising "show" on the road.

Note: If you save lots of graphics on your computer, wish to e-mail them, or simply want to organize them more efficiently, it's better to transfer them onto removable media. You can save hard drive space by compressing files. There are lots of freeware (free) and shareware (nominal fee) software programs available for download off the web to accommodate compression needs. A popular program for Windows is WinZip, which can compress and decompress various .zip files. Stuffit Deluxe and Stuffit Expander from Aladdin are popular compression programs among Mac users.

Sample Newsletter

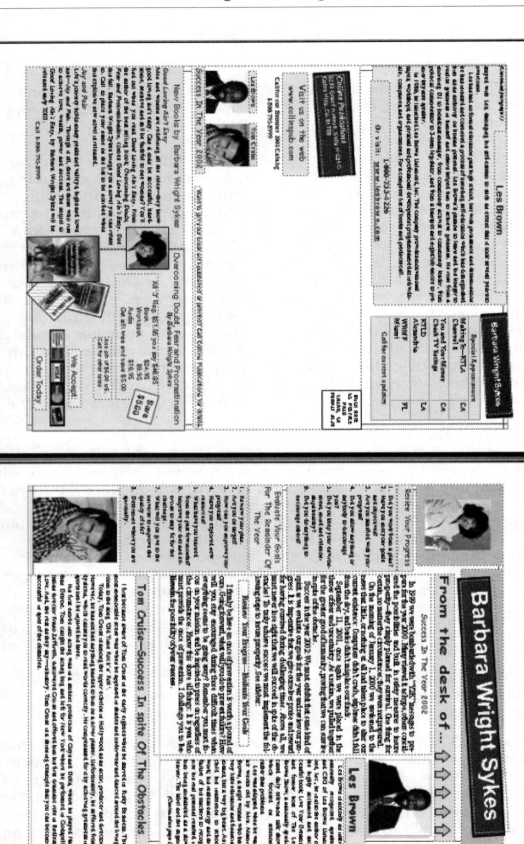

Typeset in MS Publisher

Newsletters: Newsletters are an excellent marketing tool. They allow you to update your customers on changes that are going on in your business, or perhaps progress you have made in the business. Newsletters can convey a more personal tone and allow you to reconnect with customers who perhaps haven't been "in touch" for a while.

Columns: When designing newsletters, first decide how many columns you want to use to separate the text. Most designers prefer five vertical columns or blocks, and will in fact devote only three to actual text, leaving the outer two for graphics.

Font: For the font size, select one *no smaller* than 10 points – anything smaller may be illegible for some readers. For typeface (font *style*) in the body, it is usually best to select one from the "serif" category. All fonts essentially fall into two broad categories, regardless of style: serif and sans serif. Serif includes "ornamentation," or serifs (example: Times New Roman); Sans serif is without ornamentation, hence the word *sans* (example: Arial). The reason serif is typically preferable to sans serif is because we are used to reading such copy with serif and most of us originally learned to read in serif. Consider your newspaper, a book or a magazine. Nearly all of these use serif fonts because serifs help us make out individual letters, and therefore words, more easily.

Additional: Images, headlines, and sub-headlines can successfully span all of the columns. Also, consider separating text with graphics – clip art, charts or graphs. This will give the page some welcome visual relief. Finally, remember to place large text in large columns, and smaller text in smaller columns.

Flyers: While flyers are easy to make, they're not always easy to design for maximum impact. The first thing to keep in mind when designing a flyer is "The 10-Foot Rule." The 10-Foot Rule says, if the dominant element of the piece (often the headline), be it a word, phrase, graphic or any combination, is not interesting and identifiable from 10 feet away, it's not bold enough nor big enough. Be decorative and dramatic with headlines. The most important thing is to keep it big and bold.

Once you've decided on a dominant element that is both bold and big enough, be sure to vary the look of the rest of your information. If you're including subheadings, vary the font and size to make them more interesting. Generally you will angle blocks of text only if you're not using much text. If you're including several sentences and/or paragraphs, including margins in the body is just as important for enhancing smooth reading flow, and this is more easily done if you limit visual angling.

Leave empty space for margins on all outer sides. This helps draw the reader toward the center of the page. Left justify or center dominant text, particularly if using a lot of text. Break text info easily digestible blocks and include indents and enough white space between lines for greater legibility.

General rule: devote 80% of space to "big stuff" (important phrases and graphics) and the rest to smaller, less important text (but be sure to make the smaller legible).

Callouts, or bolder, bigger and often boxed and shaded "sidebars" can be used to repeat or paraphrase a sentence or concept. They act as teasers to entice the customer into reading more of the detailed text. Such callouts can cross over into traditional margins to help them stand out. They also provide visual relief much like graphics do.

As far as white space, again, if you're going to have a lot of it, just make sure it's intentional. It should help guide the reader's eye to key elements rather than detracting from the overall message. Don't forget to include contact information, at minimum, a phone number. Check out: www.usps.gov for discounted direct mail services on flyers.

Designing a Portfolio: A good portfolio is a visual reference of your talents. There are specialties, such as home décor, where it's not feasible—and usually not possible—for you to carry your designs around with you. Of course you can show a small pillow or even bring a bedspread; however, the bedspread would show better in a photograph in the desired setting. But a visual presentation would serve to show the quality of your workmanship. A portfolio would be the perfect vehicle to showcase your designs. Chances are you have clients who would give you permission to photograph the work that you have done in their homes. A collection of such photographs will make up a great portfolio. Be sure to get a written release from the clients. If those clients are satisfied with your work, you might also consider getting testimonials as well. Samples of those forms can be found in the Home Décor forms available from Collins Publications.

How elaborate you want to make your portfolio is subject to personal preference. When I started out I simply purchased a nice white binder with a place to insert a cover sheet on the front. I used a good camera to take pictures of display pieces I made for my studio and later included designs I made for clients. I purchased nice labels from an office supply store and had the style numbers put below each picture with a small description of the fabrics used. I placed them in protector sheets and inserted them into my binder. This was some time ago. Now I have come full circle into the electronic age of computers and have so many more options available to me.

I recently worked with a client who has started a children's clothing line. She hired me as a consultant to assist in her marketing campaign. One of the very first projects we worked on was getting her business image in place. That was a lot of fun; you can do so much with children's clothing. We used primary colors by choice of my client, which proved to work well for visual presentation. She purchased a new digital camera and with a short learning curve, she was up to speed in no time. She literally had more pictures than she needed. Budget was a consideration so she, too, used the white binder for her portfolio. The nice thing about having a digital camera is you can manipulate them right from the computer so there is no need to put labels on pictures. You can add wonderful fonts to the pictures; add borders. You can do just about anything to add graphical interest. I had her purchase the best photo quality paper to print out the sheets for her binder. She had an inkjet printer that had outstanding output for pictures. You could hardly tell they weren't from a commercial printer. That made it all the better.

If you change your portfolio often to keep it current, or you design new lines frequently, I would suggest you try this approach with the binder. It is convenient, cost-effective, and it shows well.

If, on the other hand, you have the discretionary funds, you can hire a graphics designer and a photographer to put the portfolio together for you. But you must have visual representation of your business to show new prospects. You know what they say: *A picture is worth a thousand words!*

Recap: Besides marketable graphics, a good headline will be the other predominant gravitational force behind a successful ad. A headline, much like a photo, can make the ad or break it. Here are some tips on creating effective headlines. Headlines should take up between 30 and 40 percent of your ad's print space. Another 20 to 30 percent should be devoted to subheads, taglines, and/or logos. If you have fewer words, this probably means you should increase the font size. If you have a large headline, say 10 or even more words (which is ok, if words are well-chosen), resize the font accordingly, ensuring it still takes up approximately 30 to 40 percent of the space.

For font style, try to stay away from gimmicky or under-legible types. Your primary goal is to grab potential customers' attention with the use of properly sized, enticing copy, not make them rack their brain trying to make out letters. Stick with the clear and highly legible.

Content: Good headlines tend to have two components:

1) They make a factual statement (you are offering a product or service – you're creating awareness of you and your services/products)

2) They suggest a benefit to the customer (because you want them to come to *you* – you're appealing to them emotionally/socially/economically)

The factual statement is essential in any headline. Your purpose isn't just to entertain, it's to *sell*. Potential customers need to know what you're selling, and they'll prefer to know they'd be getting a bargain if they come to you; a good product at a good—if not great—price.

That's where the benefit comes in. In addition to a good product at a good price, think about what else your customer seeks when they consider giving you their business. Sometimes they're looking for more than just an economical transaction, they're seeking to achieve or maintain social status, comfort, beauty; a generally enhanced way of life. When you tell them that's what they'll get in addition to a good service, you've attracted them at both an economic and emotional level. If you can combine the two in your headline, you've got a great chance at capturing their attention.

While fact/offer + benefit (status, comfort, discount, etc.) is the most common prescription for an effective headline, there are a few variations. You may also decide to advertise as a company that's been in business for *X* number of years. This establishes a good deal of credibility and experience, and customers are drawn to that.

Another variation is keeping the headline simply news-oriented. Perhaps you are advertising sewing lessons. Such news stated simply is also an effective draw.

Brainstorm. Think about all the ways you could say something. Write and rewrite the same idea in different ways. Every word is important. Every word should be purposeful. If you persist, you will come up with compelling copy. And you will get better with more experience.

Newsletters, Flyers, Brochures, catalogs and portfolios require that you have an understanding of the principles of design in order to execute them well. This applies even if you are going to hire a professional. You must have some concept of what you are paying them for. All of your collateral pieces such as those mentioned here along with your logo, business cards, and letterhead must be in good taste. The knowledge of design elements will ensure they are.

Sample of Letterhead

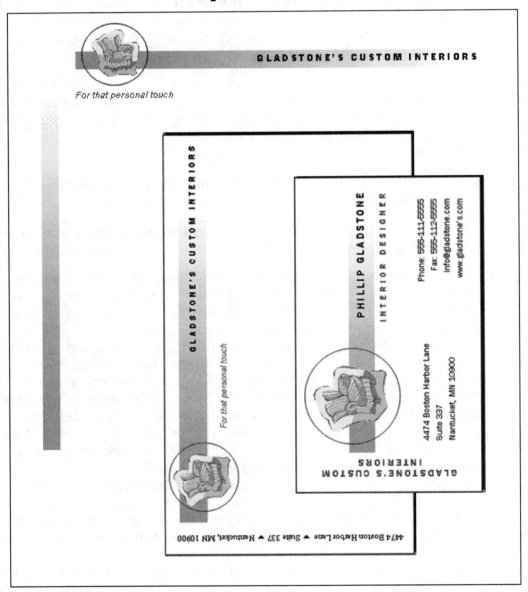

Color scheme is Marine. Design is axis busines card from Publisher. Clipart: imported chair graphis, moved, sized, and changed all font colors. Header font: Franklin gothic demi, 12 pt. Slogan: Arial 12 point. Address; franklin gothic book 7 point.

Guidelines for Designing Specific Ad Pieces

Letterhead: Letterhead is another one of those "lasting first impressions" mediums. You need to keep this in mind as you design your own letterhead. How professional your letterhead looks makes a significant impression as to how professionally you run your overall business in your readers' minds.

Letterhead is sometimes used in tandem with a company's logo, or a similar rendition of that logo. Letterhead, essentially, is the composition of your company's contact information. It includes your company name, address, telephone number, fax number, and usually nowadays, a customer service e-mail address and web site address.

Here are some tips for designing your own letterhead:

- Design your letterhead in black & white first, since you'll likely be faxing and photo-copying documents containing letterhead quite often.

- The principles of font selection for logos can also be applied to letterhead composition. Serifs and straight lines tend to convey a more traditional, serious business image while curvy fonts with fewer serifs tend to convey a more playful one. Although with extra thought, playful can still say professional. It's the overall composition that counts.

- Letterhead is commonly placed at the top center of a letter. But if you want to experiment with other placements, such as the left or right side of the top of the page, or streaming down the left column of an entire page (but print should still be horizontal, not vertical if you chose to stream down a column), this may work just as effectively. Some companies choose to devote a single full line to letterhead, running across the top of the page, others choose to separate the information into several lines, stacked one underneath the other. Experiment with several placements to see what works best.

- Proofread! Spell check does not catch all errors. Double and triple-check for spelling errors and get someone else to give a read-over as well.

- Maintain a running visual theme throughout your letterhead, business cards, envelopes, invoices, and the like, as this helps establish and maintain an identity.

- If you're including color, try limiting it to two or three, as any more can be distracting.

- Use standard sizes for paper and envelopes. (Fewer run-ins at the post office)

- Consult United States Postal Service documentation on designing letter mail for accompanying envelope specifications.

Sample of Seasonal Ad Campaign Flyer

Easter Dresses

Style: 3349

Style: 3349-A

Appointment Only

Style: 3349-B

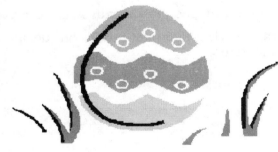

Princess Designs
1-555-555-5555
333 Durand St.
Inglewood, NJ 59909

Custom designed dresses for your little princess.

Announcements and Grand Openings

You never know what is possible until you try. Relax and have some fun announcing your new venture; after all, you should be proud.

7

Announcing Your Business

Now that you have identified your market, studied your competition, and have a clear understanding of your customer, you need to inform the public-at-large. You must bring your goods and services to their attention. Start with your immediate friends and family, business associates anyone you can think of that would benefit from your services. Make a list of those individuals and send out announcements informing them of your new business venture. Don't hesitate to ask them for names of their friends and associates who might be interested in your services. Remember in *The "Business" Of Sewing* and *Pricing Without Fear*, we said having only friends, family and neighbors was simply not enough to support a business and keep it healthy. That remains true; however, it gives you a place to start. The goal of announcing a business may not register with you as being that important, but it is vital because you need to capture the attention of your prospects, and you must stimulate their desire to conduct business with you. Get people to talk up your business to others. Start a chain reaction.

Now don't go into cardiac arrest when I make this next suggestion. Get a list of the local businesses in your community, the chamber of commerce, your local congressperson, and the address to the White House. Your list should be complete with all the associations you belong to, your alumni committee, your church, previous jobs, and just about anybody you know that is breathing! Send your announcements to all of these contacts. Be sure to include obvious businesses on your list such as vendors you currently do business with or those in the industry who should know about your business. What's so wrong with sending announcements to fabric stores? All companies should be aware of your business. Just think how sophisticated and professional they will view you and your business. Don't neglect the press. Send press releases to all the local papers, radio stations, cable stations, etc. You get the picture. For more on press releases see the chapter "Free Publicity".

The Grand Opening

This concept of having a grand opening does have impact on promoting your business, believe it or not. It is your job to stimulate excitement about your new venture. Does the grand opening have to be elaborate to be successful? No, but it must be in good taste. If you can, have a small grand opening of your business, complete with samples of your work for review. It doesn't have to be elaborate; plan on some light refreshments. The menu can be as simple or as elaborate as you want to make it. Visit your local store or one of the large warehouse centers such as Costco or Sam's Club. Make a menu as you browse their deli sections. Jot down the prices of items you feel would make for a good presentation. Get the list from the deli section at your local grocers. Better yet, get them involved by telling them what your goal is and have them suggest a menu that fits within your budget.

I worked with a sewing professional who was launching her business. I called the local university, which had a culinary arts department, and arranged a spread you would not believe for an outrageously low fee. The students in the culinary arts were eager to try their hand at a grand opening event. To this day I still cannot believe how well the whole affair turned out. It just takes a little imagination and the will to inform others of what you are doing. Many times they will get very involved and engage themselves in the process. You never know what is possible until you try. It is these kinds of experiences I hope will inspire you to try to promote your business in much the same way. Relax and have some fun announcing your new venture; after all, you should be proud. It takes a lot to start a business and run it effectively. Announcing your business and having a grand opening is one sure way of starting on the right foot.

This method is one of the non-traditional ways of promoting your business. If you run your business out of your home select a location that feels comfortable to you and has the image indicative of your business. Think, as they say, outside the box!

Sample Grand Opening Post Card

ATTRACTING THE CUSTOMER

Three basic reasons consumers buy: wants, needs and desires. Understanding consumer motivation will allow you to attract the customer.

8

Consumer Motivation

Product Reliability and Quality: Two words readily come to mind when thinking about product—reliability and durability. In speaking about quality, consumers are more inclined to buy a product or service if the quality is excellent. This is not a new phenomenon, but one that some entrepreneurs tend to forget. You have heard the old saying: "You get what you pay for." People will pay more for good quality. It is called value. If quality and product reliability are present, the consumer can easily see the value in doing business with you, and they don't mind paying for it. Because of the value principle, some people prefer to shop at Nordstrom where the sky's the limit.

One Stop Shopping, Convenience and Variety: Consumers are extremely busy and perfer to shop where they can acquire a number of products and services. They like the idea of the one-stop shopping. It saves them time, money and stress. See *Bridal and Special Occasion* in this book for a case study demonstrating this principle. Convenience comes in many ways and customers adore it. Think of ways you can make the shopping experience convenient for your customers and capitalize on it. Tip: location, method of payment, one-stop shopping, hours and days of business, and variety of products and services. It could be the one ingredient that sets you apart from your competition.

Wants, Needs, Demand and Desire: The three basic reasons why consumers buy are wants, needs and desires. Your job is to understand each. More importantly, you must understand what goods and services you have that will satiate the wants, needs and desires of the ultimate consumer. Next, you must know how to capture their attention, so that they will depart with some of those disposable or discretionary dollars and do business with you. In economics there is a philosophy called supply and demand. When a good or service is in short supply, and the demand for it is high, the price goes up. Let's say that a large corporation relocated their executives to your town and built homes for them. You are an expert in home décor and you live in a rural community where there aren't any interior decorators and few department stores that cater to the needs of the homeowner with respect to home décor. With the influx of the new homeowners and the need for your talents, coupled with the lack of adequate supply of services for their needs, it is safe to say that you are in demand. According to the law of supply and demand you are king when it comes to your pricing and getting the business.

Service: It is not enough to have an excellent product if you can't extend the one thing that seems to be overlooked, especially in our microwave society, and that is service. You have heard consumers say: "I shop there because the service is better." This element of consumer buying has never changed. It ranks right up there with quality, reliability and durability. Consumers want to receive good service, and they want the sewing professional to be just that—a professional.

Established Relationships, Sales Staff and the Entrepreneur: Customers often continue to frequent a business because they like the salesperson or the waitress or consultant. They have formed a healthy rapport with this individual and like the relationship that has developed. It makes them comfortable and secure. Customers will drive out of their way to take their business to a place where they have established a relationship. The key ingredient to establishing a good relationship with the consumer lies in the hands of the sales staff and the owner of the business. It is the job of the owner to define how the consumer is to be treated by making storewide policies regarding the service the customer should receive. The owner should always seek customer comments to determine if the level of service is meeting the needs of the ultimate consumer.

Word Of Mouth, Reputation, and Image: Service plus quality equals your reputation. What additional factors build strong image and reputation? Your ability to operate your business as a business not a hobby. Caring enough to dress professionally, completing clients' projects in a timely manner, paying attention to details, and the fact that you genuinely care about the well-being of your clients. This is what creates your image, forms a good reputation and translates into word-of-mouth recommendations regarding your business. There can be no dollar value placed upon customer loyalty garnered by a good reputation and positive business image.

Price: Price is important to certain segments of the population. Your job is to determine where the level of price resistance is. However, keeping in mind that you cannot satisfy everyone, and you are establishing your prices with a specific clientele in mind—those who can afford it! Thus, you will structure your price list and your marketing efforts to attract those clients, and you will refuse to entertain those who say you are too high.

Method of Payment: We are living in a plastic society. Virtually everyone has at least one credit card, some have so many they could qualify as collectors. When I decided to offer the use of credit cards in my business, I was astounded at how much it actually increased my profit margin. One of my very best clients said to me: "I am so glad that you accept credit cards, now I can spend more money with you!" And spend, she did. That is the best testimony I can give for the argument to offer the leading credit cards.

Coupons and Discounts: Some consumers tend to respond to these offers. However, this method of attracting consumer attention should not be overused. It should be utilized periodically, but not to the extent that you become known as a bargain-basement sewing professional.

Trends: There is a large segment of the population that follows trends, no matter whether they are trends in fashion, or trends in home décor. Keeping abreast of these trends can help you appeal to that segment and allow you to further increase your profit margin.

Style: In my experience as a sewing professional, I have identified my clients who are extremely conscious of their own personal style. These are my clients who will pay for their clothing to be made at all cost. They don't want to be duplicated; they are not trend followers. They are dissatisfied with department stores because they are limited in selection with respect to fabric, color, silhouette and design. Therefore, they seek out my services for custom tailoring. With these options available, they feel empowered, and that is valuable to them. So I capitalize on this concept in my marketing. I market to this segment of the population: the more affluent corporate executive, with lots of disposable income where money is no object. This allows me to charge higher prices because I fully understand the wants, needs and desires of my customer.

Seasons: Just as we have certain seasons of the year, there are certain goods and services that are seasonal. Planning your marketing efforts around this philosophy will give you the competitive edge. You must be careful to fill off-peak and off-season with other goods and services that can help you maintain a profit in the interim.

Society and Peer Pressure: Also known as, "keeping up with the Jones's." Throughout history man has striven to keep up with his neighbors, colleagues, family, friends, peers and society standards. Why? The answer lies in the fact that the drive is so strong to fit in; to be in the rank and file, and to be a part of the status quo. It compels us to spend money we don't even have. We want to "be, do and have" what others in society possess. Some people follow trends as though they were gospel.

Knowledge and Expertise: One of fastest ways to become obsolete in the marketplace is to fail to keep your knowledge and expertise current. Your clients come to you because you are the expert, and they are willing to pay you for your knowledge and expertise. In a business where you provide a service or consultation, such as a sewing business, your knowledge and expertise regarding your field of specialty is more apparent. Working in close contact with the client makes it easier to sense whether you know what you are doing. Customer confidence and their willingness to pay you what you are worth requires that you maintain your knowledge and skill level at all times.

Obsolescence: In my marketing classes, I learned that some manufacturers make products with obsolescence in mind. It works in their favor because it gives the consumer a need to repeatedly do business with them. For instance, let's say you are a manufacturer of eight-track tapes. Now, when you first planned the eight-track tape you also planned the cassette tape. Your strategy was to introduce the eight tracks, and entice all the major manufacturers of electronic stereo devices to offer them in their units. Furthermore, you had set a specific time frame for the life cycle of the eight-track. It would last three years prior to the introduction of the cassette tape, with eventual phase out of the eight tracks, making the eight tracks become completely obsolete. Your job is to watch the market and offer products that satisfy obsolescence. Perhaps in your business you will have a product life cycle with a replacement in mind. The computer industry is notorious for doing this. Where is the 286 CPU? Or the first floppy disk? Did someone mention DVD?

Brand Awareness: Some consumers buy, not because the product has been tried and proven effective—at least not by them. They buy because they have been made aware of that brand. We are programmed through repetitious, subliminal advertising. A customer could be standing in the middle of the aisle pondering a bath soap purchase, never having tried any of the available brands on the shelf: he or she will purchase the one with the most famous brand recognition. Consumer philosophy chants: "I've heard of it, so it must be good!"

Economy and Disposable Income: In a stable economy where the dollar is strong, interest rates are low, unemployment is down; consumer confidence tends to be high. Not to mention that consumers have more disposable income and are eager to part with it. You find purchases of clothing and household articles at an all-time high. These are times where you are least likely to experience price resistance. People feel less intimidated in spending on leisure and luxury items. This could represent a prime opportunity for you to market and capture the attention of the more affluent consumer.

Comfortable Environment: I had a client once who told me—in the middle of a fitting—that she enjoys doing business with me because my office and my sewing studio were so comfortable. She liked the décor, lighting and the privacy. I operate my custom tailoring business out of my home. She said that there are some places that make her uncomfortable, and she refuses to shop there no matter how good the price may be. In fact, she shared that when she was in Cleveland she had gone to a sewing professional who had been recommended to her because she was so reasonable (cheap). She had gone there with high expectations. The lady came to the door dressed like a bag lady... the place was a wreck! It was early in the afternoon and the her children running around unsupervised. My client said she didn't care how reasonable the lady was, she wanted her shopping experience to feel good. She stated that she didn't book the project and never returned to do business with her.

Distribution: This applies mainly to businesses where they rely upon others to make their products available to the public. If you rely upon this form of doing business, it is imperative that your distribution channels be in place prior to starting any marketing, advertising or promotions campaign. If you are selling wholesale, distribution could be a key factor in positioning your products in the marketplace. You could lose clients by advertising that products are sold and available, when in fact they are not available due to poor distribution efforts.

E-Commerce: I never thought I would be able to sit at home and do all my shopping from a computer. The Internet has opened a whole new shopping and business experience. However, in a sewing business I still prefer to have face-to-face contact with my clients. There is something so surreal about making a project for someone whom you have never fitted or personally taken measurements for. I am not saying it can't be done. I have worked with my colleagues to take measurements of my clients who live in other geographical locations. There are a number of sewing professionals that conduct business in this manner and love not having the client present. In defense of this new wave of business, it does work. A web presence is absolutely necessary to participate in e-commerce. Consumer confidence has risen and people are less fearful of placing orders on the Internet which require leaving credit card information. When I attended a Tech-Net meeting at Microsoft last November, one of the consultants said that eventually we will not have to leave our homes for anything. We can shop through e-commerce and even find a mate and get married all on the Internet. I guess anything is possible since we can now do our banking and have our clothes cleaned from a grocery store. The possibilities are endless!

Marketing, Advertising and Promotions: I can't help but say it again: How in the world did "big" companies get to be "big?" How about "Marketing, Advertising and Promotions?" A well-thought out and executed plan can put your goods and services before the attention of millions of consumers. It can influence what they think and how they think about you and your goods and service. It can change a "want" into a need. The right campaign can create demand. With some degree of planning and market manipulation you can force the price to increase. Case in point: Elmo, Cabbage Patch, Furbies, and Beanie Babies, are just a few products that have enjoyed price increase and market demand as a result of a brilliant promotional campaign. Brand and product awareness are also spawned through the use of a strategic campaign. There are two types of methods to consider when planning your marketing, advertising and promotional campaign; traditional and non-traditional. The latter is more cost effective.

Marketing Model

9

Remember, most people are asking themselves: "What's in it for me?" Don't wait for them to guess. Tell them.

Marketing Model Description

This model is especially helpful in your marketing campaigns and for working with businesses that share a customer in common with you, as well as calling warm and cold leads. See Call Planning Worksheet for preparing your script for the call and the Customer Contact Form for making and reporting your call results.

How does this benefit you as a sewing professional?

You can put together a flyer and have the other business include it into their mailing to their customers. In certain situations you can pool your resources and do what is called co-operative advertising through direct mail or e-mail marketing campaigns. Or, you can simply exchange client lists.

Step One: Finding the Leads

The first step would be to identify as many businesses as you can. Make sure they have a strong emphasis in your customer. Find out how many customers they have if possible. Consequently, they can better appreciate the need for your services. Once you have established which businesses are appropriate for targeting, it's time to draft a letter introducing yourself and your services briefly. I say briefly because you will go into detail in your face-to-face meeting with them later. In your letter you would follow our standard format of keeping it to one page. Tell them you will follow-up with a phone call within seven business days to set the appointment. Make sure you stipulate that you only want 15 minutes of their time. Most people do not mind sparing 15 minutes to meet with you. You will clearly state your purpose and the benefits to them.

How to find leads:
1. Yellow Pages
2. Internet, using keywords related to the business you are searching for
3. Directory of Associations
4. Your vendors

Step Two: Writing the Letter

How to write the letter:
1. Open with the introduction of you and your business.
2. State a fact that demonstrates you understand their business.
3. Go directly to the benefits for them.
    a. Open with a sizzle: Tell them you have customers you can refer to them. (Use as a carrot)
    b. Create the demand to meet with you by stating you have additional benefits you would like to discuss in a face-to-face meeting.
4. Tell them you only desire 15 minutes.
5. Tell them you will call in seven business days to set up the meeting.
6. Close with enthusiasm and demand for you.
    a. "I look forward to meeting with you to explore how we may be of mutual benefit to each other."
    b. "I look forward to meeting with you to share how I can be of benefit to your business."

Step Three: The Phone Call

The phone call is made usually around a time that most business people are receptive to entertaining calls. I have found that between 9 am and 10 am work best for me. Generally people have arrived, had a chance to get their morning coffee and are in the frame of mind to take care of business. As a rule, most people expect calls during that time. Never call a new prospect at 8 am, 12 noon, or after 3 pm. Those seem to be shutdown modes for most individuals for obvious reasons: At eight in the morning most people are just walking in the door and the sound of someone on the other end of a phone before they have had a chance to settle in is annoying. Likewise, for the noon hour they are focusing on taking their lunch break and their concentration is next to none. At three in the afternoon they are wrapping up loose ends, closing out their day and planning for tomorrow. So be mindful of the optimum calling times and use them wisely. After all, you want the person on the other end to be receptive to your call.

Once you have them on the line, don't beat around the bush. Get straight to the point. Remember, this is not a cold call. You have already gotten your foot in the door by the letter you sent. This is your leverage so use it wisely. Introduce yourself with your name followed by the name of your business. Refresh their memory by saying you promised to call to set an appointment for only 15 minutes to meet with them. Be sure to capitalize on the fact that both of you have the same customer in common and that this is why it would be beneficial for the two of you to meet.

Also remember, most people are asking themselves: *What's in it for me?* Don't leave them to guess—tell them. Once you have set the appointment, don't forget to let them know you are enthusiastic about meeting with them. You can convey enthusiasm without sounding phony or overly anxious. Example: "I look forward to meeting with you next Wednesday at ten." Always restate the meeting date and time before you close. It helps them to focus on what they have just committed to.

Don't make idle conversation after that. It's time to bring the phone conversation to a close. Plus, it makes you look professional and someone who is adept at taking care of business. First impressions are crucial; so don't diminish yours by overstaying your welcome. If you can't state your purpose in a timely manner and you tend to babble on, chances are you will not have the capability to keep a face-to-face interview within the time limit you requested. So don't blow it by letting nervous tension overtake you. Rehearse your presentation the night before you call. You will find that rehearsing is an excellent antidote for nervous tension.

Tips for making the phone call:

1. Rehearse the night before.
2. During the call:
   a. Introduce you and your company.
   b. Refresh their memory by referring to the letter you sent.
   c. Restate the reason for the call.
   d. Go directly to the benefits.
   e. Remind them it's only for 15 minutes.
   f. Close with enthusiasm and restate meeting date and time.
3. Be sure to mark your day planner and three-month calendar.

Step Four: The Meeting

The meeting is where you shine. Chances are, the entrepreneur has never considered the benefit of working with a sewing professional. It's your job to introduce the concept and give it merit as it relates to them. Remember you already know what you want and how the relationship between the two of you will be profitable for both parties. If you keep in the forefront of your mind the fact that you must convey these benefits, you will execute your presentation with clarity and purpose. There is nothing more frustrating for someone than to have their time wasted because you cannot accurately explain why you feel it is important for them to do business with you.

Be sure to state the fact that you are fully aware of the needs of *their* customers as they relate to the goods and services you both have to offer. Tell them (while showing them your designs) that you have an excellent line that would meet the needs of their customers. As you see them become more excited about the prospect of doing business with you, entertain their comments. Once they have an appreciation for your knowledge and expertise, it is time to explain to them how you envision the two of you being a benefit to each other. You would start by covering the following points:

How putting together a flyer that can be included in mailings to their customers works. Explain how the two of you can pool your resources and do co-operative advertising through direct mail or e-mail marketing campaigns. Tell them that because you both have the same customer in common you would be happy to exchange client lists. And don't forget to leave room for them to participate by saying, "I am also open to any suggestions you might have."

After establishing what you feel would work best for them, initiate a start date to make it all happen. If it is a flyer, tell them you will start on the initial draft right away. Ask for their input after you have put something together. Keep in mind we are still under a 15-minute deadline. If you sense they are raring to go and it appears the meeting may exceed the allotted time, tell them immediately you wouldn't mind extending the time so that the two of you could rough out a sketch. "Mr. Smith it appears that we are almost out of time. We only have five minutes left; however, I would be delighted to extend the time so we may continue to work on the flyer." The idea is to always keep their time in mind. It shows that you are truly a professional, and, more important, you respect their time. This will give them the confidence needed to turn their customers over to you. After all, they have worked hard to get their customers and they don't want to refer just anybody to them.

When you close, do so with a follow-up time and date to show the initial sketch for the flyer. Or, it may be to come together for a focus meeting to move forward on your agreement. No matter the purpose, it's your job to take charge and move things along. Never, ever forget to thank them for their time.

Tips for the meeting:
1. Rehearse the day before.
2. Take your business cards, flyers, portfolio, and sample pieces.
3. Make your presentation with clarity and purpose.
4. Show samples and your portfolio as you talk.
5. Enlist their comments as they show enthusiasm.
6. Tell them your plan of action.
    a. Direct Mail
    b. E-mail Marketing
    c. Co-op Advertising
    d. Customer List Exchange
7. Convey the benefits.
8. Leave room for them to make suggestions.
9. Initiate the first effort to provide a concept or sketch, etc.
10. Acknowledge the time. (If the meeting is running past 15 minutes)
11. Make the appointment for the follow-up or focus meeting.
12. Thank them for their time.

Writing Your Letter

Use the form on the next page to assist you in writing your letter. Plug in the sentences under each heading. Use *Dissecting the Letter,* as a guide to help you formulate your sentences. Yours doesn't have to be exactly like the example, but should meet the objectives outlined. As you write each sentence, try to put yourself in the recipient's place. Ask yourself what would move you to want to do business, or even entertain an appointment, with this individual. That should get your thought processes flowing.

Refer to the list of words that sell if you get stuck. Also, keep your dictionary and thesaurus handy for easy reference. Practice saying the sentences out loud to see if they make sense to you. Often we can't recognize distorted sentence flow until we verbalize them. If you find that you have hit a brick wall, change the orientation of where you are writing. By that I mean move to another part of your office or even to another location altogether. There may be something distracting you in that present locale.

What can you do if you find you can't finish the letter in one sitting? First of all, don't get upset. Rome wasn't built in a day. It might be a good idea to leave it for a moment, and return when you are refreshed. Take a coffee break and do something that doesn't relate to the letter at all. Take a walk or read something humorous. Chances are you have become too stressed out over the letter and need to step back and take a breather. It happens to the best of us. Don't let it throw you; just acknowledge that you need a break and let it be. When you return to it, you will be better for having done so.

Template for the Body of the Letter

1. Open with the introduction of you and your business.

2. State a fact that demonstrates you understand their business.

3. Go directly to the benefits for them. Open with the sizzle: Tell them you have customers you can refer to them. (Use as a carrot)

4. Create the demand to meet with you by stating that you have additional benefits you would like to discuss with them in a face-to-face meeting.

5. Tell them you only desire 15 minutes. Tell them you will call in 7 business days to set up the meeting.

6. Close with enthusiasm and demand for you.

Marketing Model Outline

Step One: How to find leads

1. Yellow Pages
2. Internet, using keywords related to the business you are searching for.
3. Directory of Associations
4. Your vendors

Step Two: Writing the Letter

How to write the letter:

1. Open with the introduction of you and your business.
2. State a fact that demonstrates you understand their business.
3. Go directly to the benefits for them.
4. Open with the sizzle: Tell them you have customers you can refer to them. (Use as a carrot)
5. Create the demand to meet with you by stating that you have additional benefits you would like to discuss with them in a face-to-face meeting.
6. Tell them you only desire fifteen minutes.
7. Tell them you will call in 7 business days to set up the meeting.
8. Close with enthusiasm and demand for you.
9. "I look forward to meeting with you to explore how we may be of mutual benefit to each other."
10. "I look forward to meeting with you to share how I can be of benefit to your business."

Step Three: The Phone Call

Tips for making the phone call:

1. Rehearse the night before.
2. During the call:
    a. Introduce you and your company;
    b. Refresh their memory by referring to the letter you sent
    c. Restate the reason for the call.
    d. Go directly to the benefits.
    e. Remind them it's only for fifteen minutes.
    f. Close with enthusiasm and restate meeting date and time.
3. Be sure to mark your day planner and three-month calendar.

Step Four: The Meeting

Tips for the meeting:

1. Rehearse the day before.
2. Take your business cards, flyers, portfolio, and sample pieces.
3. Make your presentation with clarity and purpose.
4. Show samples and your portfolio as you talk.
5. Enlist their comments as they show enthusiasm.
6. Tell them your plan of action.
    a. Direct Mail
    b. E-mail Marketing
    c. Co-op Advertising
    d. Customer List Exchange.
7. Convey the benefits.
8. Leave room for them to make suggestions.
9. Initiate the first effort to provide a concept or sketch, etc.
10. Acknowledge the time. (If the meeting is running past 15 minutes)
11. Make the appointment for the follow-up or focus meeting.
12. Thank them for their time.

SAMPLE LETTER

Armstrong's Bridal and Formal Designs

Ph: 555-555-5555
Fax: 555-222-2222

123 Montclair Lane
New Vista, CA 99999

November 26, 2003

Dear Ms. Latham:

My name is Kathleen Armstrong, owner of Armstrong's Bridal and Formal Designs. I have been in business for ten years and have a clientele that takes frequent cruises throughout the year. I have designed formal attire for the Captain's Ball, and other cruise affairs. I am very familiar with the needs of your customers who also enjoy taking cruises and having the appropriate attire.

I have a list of socially elite clients that can definitely benefit from your services. *Since we have the same type of customer in common*, I would be delighted to share my contacts with you.

I also have additional ideas that I feel would benefit your business. I would like to set an appointment with you to discuss these opportunities in person. The meeting will only take 15 minutes of your time, as I appreciate the fact that you are very busy. I will call you in seven business days to set up the meeting.

I look forward to meeting with you to explore how we may be of mutual benefit to each other. In the meantime, should you have any questions, please call me at: 555-555-5555.

Sincerely,

Kathleen Armstrong
Armstrong's Bridal and Formal Designs

www.armstrongsdesigns.com   armstrong@mybiz.com

Dissecting the Letter

Did you...

Open with the introduction of you and your business?

"My name is Kathleen Armstrong, owner of Armstrong's Bridal and Formal Designs."

State a fact that demonstrates you understand their business?

"I have designed formal attire for the Captain's Ball, and other cruise affairs. I am very familiar with the needs of your customers who also enjoy taking cruises having the appropriate attire."

Go directly to the benefits for them? Open with the sizzle: Tell them you have customers you can refer to them. (Use as a carrot)

"I have a list of socially elite clients that can definitely benefit from your services. Since we have the same type of customer in common, I would be delighted to share my contacts with you."

Create the demand to meet with you by stating that you have additional benefits you would like to discuss with them in a face-to-face meeting?

"I also have additional ideas that I feel would benefit your business."

Tell them you only desire 15 minutes? Tell them you will call in seven business days to set up the meeting.

"I would like to set an appointment with you to discuss these opportunities in person. The meeting will only take 15 minutes of your time, as I appreciate the fact that you are very busy. I will call you in seven business days to set up the meeting."

Close with enthusiasm and demand for you?

"I look forward to meeting with you to explore how we may be of mutual benefit to each other. In the meantime, should you have any questions, please call me at: 555-555-5555."

Calling Warm and Cold Leads

Use the marketing model to assist you in contacting leads and current customers. In the new *Marketing Forms* available from Collins Publications, is the *Call Planning Worksheet* and the *Customer Contact Form*. These forms are especially helpful in monitoring results, garnering sales after an advertising campaign, and for planning and reporting the results of calls.

Marketing Ideas for a Sewing Business

10

Seasons are always a popular way to entice customers to spend. In August – Start planning your ad campaign for Halloween. For Fall – Capitalize on children going back to school.

Below are examples of the leads available to sewing professionals in the disciplines listed. Review the list and develop a list of your own that pertains to your specific business and your customers. It will help you think of how you should market your business. Some leads may not seem so obvious in terms of how to use them; others speak for themselves. We will examine how to use some of these leads for the various businesses. Consider each lead and how you may transfer that same philosophy into your business.

Marketing, advertising and promotions involves getting creative and innovative in your approach. Think about the design process as you move forward in this chapter. Read the elements of design, if you haven't already, and consider what is involved in designing your ad piece. Think about the message you want to convey. Study the model for writing a letter to contacts. While you are pondering the many possibilities jot down every thought that pops into your head. They are jewels and may not come back, so don't miss a valuable opportunity by neglecting to write them down.

Most Effective Methods for Generating Customer Leads

1. Word of Mouth -This is one of the best sources for customer leads. These leads are generated not only when you get out there and personally promote your business with your everyday contacts (doctor's office staff, hair salon, banker, etc...,) but also when satisfied customers tell friends and family about their experience with your business.

2. Community Involvement - When you're involved in community events, you're more visible – more people get to know you and you can tell them about your business.

3. Product Literature - Suppliers' literature about their products and services helps spread the message that you're in business and what you sell in a clear and concise manner.

4. Directory Ads – Directory ads designed for your trade community often rank among the top three most effective ways to generate customer inquiries and sales.

5. Newspaper Ads – Newspaper ads rank high in effectiveness, not far behind a directory ad's value.

6. Newsletters – Let your customers know what you're up to, what's new, and any promotions you're running. Keeping them in the know is a good reinforcement technique.

7. Storefront Signage – Simply affixing the business name in front of your store will entice walk-ins.

8. Seminars and How-To Clinics – Offer day-long or weekend-long classes teaching your skills to interested others.

9. Publicity Releases - See "Free Money for Marketing and PR."

10. Theme Sales – You can center your campaign on a theme to make it interesting. For example, you sell furniture with an Asian motif; your ad piece would reflect that as well. Your campaign may also be directed toward that consumer. See the Advertising example in the chapter "Home Décor."

11. Seasons – This is always a popular way to get customers to respond. When you plan your campaign around a season build in enough time to develop and distribute your sales piece. For Fall: Capitalize on kids going back to school. Mark your calendar in August to start planning your ad campaign for Halloween.

12. Events – Every year in March I use *National Procrastinators' Week* to promote my book *Overcoming Doubt, Fear and Procrastination*. Not only does it help sell that book, it also helps bring my work in the sewing industry to the attention of the ultimate consumer. Use events wisely and they can really help, even if they are related to something else you are doing.

Non-Traditional Marketing Methods

Each field of sewing specialty has a uniquely built-in audience or customer. Now that you know who your customer is, it will be easy to utilize the methods we will discuss. You will need several important items:

    a. Portfolio (see *Designing A Portfolio*),
    b. Business cards and letterhead (see *Designing Elements*)
    c. Flyers, brochures or catalogs (see *Designing Elements*)
    d. Samples of your best work

Start by selecting from suggested leads below and send a letter introducing yourself, stating you will follow up with a phone call to arrange an interview. On the day of the interview take your portfolio, business cards, flyers, brochures or catalogs and a few of your best samples. During the interview you will briefly introduce yourself and the services you offer. Before concluding the interview, be specific about the nature of the visit. Tell them the benefits they will receive by embracing your business. This is known as asking for the business.

To learn more on how to write the letter, make the call and what to do during the interview see *Marketing Model* in this text.

The following are a few proven ideas to help you launch a very successful non-traditional marketing and advertising campaign using very little capital. Many of these contacts can be found in your phone directory. There are other methods that will be discussed, and some of the following methods will be expanded on throughout this text.

Marketing Ideas

Associations: For instance, if you are specializing in custom tailoring and you want to reach businesswomen in your community, you could rent the list for mass mailing purposes, or place an advertisement to attract their members.

    a. Write an article in their newsletter or bulletin highlight your services.
    b. Offer to give a brief presentation or fashion show to their members.
    c. Rent their mailing list for a direct mail campaign.

Athletic departments: Some high schools need someone to sew and alter cheerleader costumes; you should be the one to fill that void.
Bowling Leagues and Teams: If you specialize in embroidery you would definitely want to contact these organizations. They often need names and logos embroidered on the uniforms.

Business-to-Business: Network with retail establishments where you do not directly compete but share the same customer. For example, you specialize in drapery; you would network with someone who does upholstery or does carpeting. Specialize in bridal gowns? Network with photographer, jeweler or florist.

Canvassing areas: Look in the newspaper for new home developments. New home owners always need the services of sewing professionals specializing in home décor. Hire a teenager to canvass the area.

Childcare centers: Contact administrators of day care facilities and offer to give a small fashion show or just leave your flyers/brochures and business cards at the front desk in attractive Lucite stand.

Church: Connie Amaden-Crawford has a line of clothing for full-figure women. She markets her line to churches because according to her market research a great number of her customers frequent churches. See *The "Business" Of Sewing* Vol. 2: "Profile Of A Sewing Professional."

Cleaners: For those who specialize in alterations the cleaners' market has always proved to be beneficial.

Consignment: This is placing your work into retail establishments where you can earn income—as I say, even as you sleep! Contact the owner and negotiate a contract. For more in detail about consignment see my book: *Do You Sew For Profit: A Guide for Wholesale, Retail and Consignment.*

Drama departments: If you specialize in custom design, it would be wise to contact the heads of school drama departments.

Fabric stores: Offer to sew display items for the stores, and be sure that the managers allow you to get credit for your work. Ask if you can leave your flyers/brochures at the front desk and if you can put your card in their directory. Don't forget to inquire as to whether they will allow you to teach classes. Find out if they have a mailing list you could take advantage of as well.

Home Parties: Several sewing professionals who specialize in lingerie have been using home parties for years to market their line. They get the homeowner's friends to model and give a free gift to both in exchange for their participation. They can be a lot of fun. Another idea for those who market lingerie is to network with those who specialize in bridal, and have presentations during the bride's shower. There are always plenty of women who love beautiful lingerie.

Organizations and Clubs: Contact the chairperson of the organizations that would be most interested in your services. Get leads from the Encyclopedia of

Prom Coordinators: Contact the high school's prom coordinator nine months ahead and ask if you can give a brief presentation to their students. Or have them include your materials in their mailings to the parents.

Real Estate Managers: If you specialize in home décor arrange to give a brief presentation to the agents/brokers and leave your literature. Offer to exchange leads with the agents as well.

Sewing and Vacuum Companies: Many have newsletters and brochures they mail to their customers. Some customers that can't sew buy machines and would welcome the opportunity to learn.

  a. Offer to write articles in exchange for an ad about your business.
  b. Consider buying their mailing list to announce you offer sewing lessons. This would be an excellent way of getting your message out and gain additional revenue.

Sewing Professionals: Networking with other sewing professionals provides you with the opportunity to increase your client base by sharing leads with your fellow associates. If you specialize in children's clothing you will receive these referrals from your peers.

Telemarketing: Use the Marketing Model, Call Planning Worksheet and the Customer Contact Form to contact leads and current customers (See the *Marketing Model* chapter). This is especially helpful as you seek to monitor results and garner sales after an advertising campaign.

Television and Movie Studios: These businesses travel with complete sets to different locations and have need of good sewing professionals; it would be wise to send them information about you and your business.

Trunk Shows: Justine Limpus Parish has an art-to-wear business. She has been enormously successful in marketing her business through trunk shows.

We've just analyzed a number of non-traditional methods of marketing your sewing business. These are just a few of the many ways to conduct a successful cost-effective marketing and advertising campaign. That's the beauty of these ideas—they're fairly inexpensive. You can make your own list by thinking of all the different businesses and organizations that would be interested in your goods and services and follow the same steps. No matter how large or small your sewing business may be, an effective marketing, advertising and promotions campaign can lead to your success. For more help see "Identify, Profile and Demand."

FREE MARKETING MONEY

11

Solicit funding from all the companies that would benefit from having you use and talk about their products.

Millions of dollars from suppliers go unused by sewing professionals each year, largely due to the fear of rejection, disbelief that anyone would agree to give money to their business, and of course, the paperwork hassles associated with participation agreements. Free marketing co-op dollars are waiting for you and your business. Make sure to check with the supplier or their representatives. Many suppliers have relaxed their participation requirements in recent years, and this could end up saving you lots of money on advertising. So put aside your doubts and fears, and stop procrastinating. Go for it.

First Step: Review the marketing model and go over how to write a pitch letter. In the model it doesn't refer to writing the letter as such, but that's what they call it in the PR industry. Follow the guidelines set forth in the model. Here are some additional ideas to assist you in you endeavor.

Scenario: You are a sewing professional who specializes in art-to-wear, you have a book you recently wrote and have developed a lesson plan to teach courses from your text and years of experience in the industry. You are in a good place. You can teach sewing as well as art with respect to how to paint on fabric. Who would you target for free marketing money? Well, in this case the list can be developed from two industries: sewing and painting. Look at all the vendors that supply you with the products, paints, brushes, textiles, trims and so on. Now you have branded yourself well, using a clever slogan and sophisticated logo. Your marketing pieces have garnered you a great deal of notoriety in the industry from both students and clients. You have your line at major boutiques across the country and have an impressive academic background. You are indeed well-branded in both the sewing and arts industries.

Action Shots for Teaching Funds: Make sure you have action shots of yourself teaching. You need one with the audience focused on you. This shows consumer interest. It will also help your collateral pieces create demand on the part of your suppliers.

Action Shots for Other Funds: Follow the same principles. You need to have a picture of yourself in motion with the product/s of the corporation you are trying to attract. For example, a full shot of you at the sewing machine with their product, or one of your clients wearing the finished design made from the textile mill you are trying to engage. You get the picture.

Planning and Execution: Now it's time to package everything in your presentation in such a way that the full weight of your message is instantly understood by both of your core audiences. Be sure to solicit funding from all the companies that would benefit from having you use and talk about their products. If you hit a blank, think back. Take a look at all the magnificent pieces you have sewn or designed. List all the vendors you purchased from or whose products you have used to produce these items. Follow the basic marketing model outlined in this text. Take your photographs or portfolio to show what you have done using their products and put together an overview of your audience and their buying habits. Make sure you tie them into the company's customer profile to show relevance. Talk about the potential sales that are possible as a result of your representing them. If you will conduct lectures, seminars or workshops call their attention to the ongoing benefits that will be derived from this venture. Also, sell them on the fact that you would essentially be their spokesperson. And certainly a financial investment in you would enhance their visibility and increase their sales to vertical as well as horizontal markets. Be sure to use that same phrase.

The importance of your ability to capture more than one type of customer should be emphasized. Let's not overlook the fact that you have such an impressive background and your presence commands attention. If you package your presentation properly this is what they will think about you: Your work and reputation in the industry have evoked a call to action on the part of those exposed to you, and therefore have inspired them to buy items you use, suggest or make. This is what your package and presentation must convey to the suppliers.

When you put together the package, include as many articles and news clippings of you and your business as possible. Say something that is factual about their business as it relates to you or your business. Example: "Because of the excellent chemical composition of your paints, I find that the integrity of my fabrics is maintained and the feel of the fabric remains luxurious to the touch."

Asking for Funding: Finally, we must ask for the funding. Be specific about your needs and the timelines and deadlines in which the capital would be needed. Do not wait for them to ask. Tell them you would need permission to use their logo on all collateral pieces associated with personal appearances, workshops and seminars funded by them.

Once you have an agreement, ask that they use your logo and picture on their site and put a link to your site from theirs. Tell them you will reciprocate as well. The picture will be an action shot of you using their products on both sites. Tell them you would be pleased to come to them to get it done. On your site, you will have pictures of yourself holding their product while standing with one of their company representatives.

Exclusivity: Get the issue of exclusivity out of the way so that each party is clear on that point. This way if you want to solicit other companies, you are free to do so. If they want you to sign an exclusive with them, the percentage of participation will have to speak to that kind of a commitment. Be a good negotiator, especially if they want you to be exclusive to their corporation. In your contract all the key aspects will be pointed out before signing.

DIRECT MAIL

Direct mail is one avenue you should not pass up.

12

What comes to mind when you think or hear the words *direct mail?* If you think, *junk mail,* perhaps it's time to modify your thinking. One of the most important things you can do for your marketing campaign is adjust that notion and understand it as a wonderful way to communicate your message to the ultimate consumer. In fact, it is one of the best mediums to use if you desire immediate and accurate feedback on the success of your campaign. If you receive a direct mail piece for an item or service you have been anticipating, that very piece of mail becomes one of the most important things you can get. With discounted production and postal costs available to businesses, direct mail is one avenue you should not pass up.

Steps in Planning: *Determine Your Goal and/or Your Offer*

Name recognition/brand awareness	Introduction to your business
Promote a new item or service	Announcement of a special event
Reach a particular audience	Expand your customer base
Appreciation to customers	Prospects for new business
inquiry or referral	Recognize a special event

Once you have determined your goal and/or offer, you need to consider the audience you will target, which brings us to the next step.

Determine Your Target Audience

All advertising should be as targeted as possible. If you seek to reach a select group from your current list, you are engaging in what is called "narrow casting." In any case, start by combing through your current customer list and eliminate non-prospects wherever you can. Non-prospects are those customers whom you are fairly certain would just not entertain your offer. While you want to reach as many prospects as possible, you also don't want to waste precious production costs and time on those who you know will simply toss the piece into the trash. Perhaps they have already purchased this item from you.

Once you have determined the most promising audience from you list, you may decide to expand the list by renting or buying a mailing list from an outside direct mail broker. Brokers may often sell address lists per hundred or per thousand as well as quality and specifics you want. The more specific you want your list, the more the cost per name will be. When working with the list broker, ask if they have any introductory offers or specials you may take advantage of. Ask if they have any provisions for testing the list and what is the compensation to you for any returns you may receive from names purchased. That means that if you buy 100 names from them and 20 come back, will they reimburse you; if so, at what percentage of returns will this be applicable.

These are key concerns since mailing costs time and money for planning, design, printing and postage, plus the list fee. They should keep their list clean. That is part of their job as list brokers, not yours. Ask them if they can provide the list on disks and in what format and how do they send the disk to you. A common format for list brokers is Excel, which is a Microsoft program. I don't know of a print house or mail fulfillment house that doesn't honor this program. Fulfillment or mailing services are also an option you may consider. Some of them offer lists and will provide all the needed services to you as well—at a cost, of course.

Brokers can be contacted using the Yellow Pages under Mailing List Brokerage Firms or you can search the 'net for a firm of your choice. Use key words such as: List Brokers or Mailing Lists

Cater Your Promotional Material Accordingly

Now that you have decided on a list, it's time to design your material. At this point, you know what you want to say and whom you are to say it to. This should make the design and copy decisions relatively easy. Besides clearly communicating services and products with proper copy and cohesive graphics (if they apply), you should also include an incentive for the customer to reply to the offer or announcement (a coupon for instance; a reply card or a rebate of some kind ... be creative). Be sure to include offer and incentive details on your reply mechanism if it is a separate piece.

You don't need to succumb to the intimidation that can be brought on by seeing larger companies' marketing materials. While color and good copy do matter, the most important pieces of the puzzle are getting your message out clearly to the ones who will most likely respond. You have a service or product, and they need to know about it. If you want to convey an image of sophistication, consider that in your total design. If you want to express a more light-hearted, fun message or announcement, detail that in your design. Perhaps you want to suggest the feeling of a personal letter; then write in such a way. Consider using customer testimonials if possible. It's important that you communicate what you want clearly and concisely with an element of tantalization in order to generate the desired response.

Track Your Results

Finally, keep a record of your direct mail campaign results. When you've done something right and get a desired response, you want to know what exactly it was you did so you can repeat it. Track offer information, copy and design, incentive and feedback statistics and compare campaigns. Study the successful ones and continue to use them.

A key to your success is your attitude. And that applies to your view of direct mail as well. If you've traditionally considered direct mail as "junk mail," make it a priority to replace that negative notion with a more productive one.

Direct Mail Marketing Checklist	
Completed	*What kind of list(s) am I using?* Do you want to reach a general audience using all your customers? Or do you want to target a selected segment (narrow cast)? You must know your audience before you proceed further.
□Yes □No	
□Yes □No	*What is my offer?* An open house/party for new services/business? A new product or line? A special sale? Rebates? Coupons?
□Yes □No	*Is the offer or announcement stated clearly in the headline and/or opening sentences?*
□Yes □No	*Is the offer compelling enough to grab the reader in 5 seconds?*
□Yes □No	*Does the product or service need an explanation?* If so, use the direct mail piece as an opening educational tool on that product/service.
□Yes □No	*Can I offer anything FREE?* (A free product, brochure, consultation, catalog, etc. has a tantalizing appeal.)
□Yes □No	*What tone is used in the copy?* Using a personal tone will make it more readable.
□Yes □No	*Have I written using the customer's perspective?*
□Yes □No	*How will the customer get in touch with me?* Have you included business telephone number, address, e-mail, and/or web site information – on the primary piece or on a separate reply card?
□Yes □No	*Is the piece cohesive, and the message consistent?* Do graphics logically agree with the message you're sending in the copy? Does headline information agree with any support copy?

Online Mailing

The United States Postal Service (USPS) offers a service called Online Mailing which has a discounted postage rate. This is an excellent service to take advantage of to save you time and money on your marketing campaign and other correspondence. You can design such pieces as flyers, newsletters, catalogs, postcards and booklets – or have someone do it for you. Rates are nearly unbeatable as they not only include preparation and production, but postage as well. Plus you don't have to do any traveling – everything can be done on your desktop computer. The postal service can upload your recipient address information into their system and take care of nearly everything else once you have decided on a design and quantities. For example:

Say you want to create and send 200 8½ by 11 black-and-white one-page flyers stuffed in individual envelopes. The total cost would be $100.20. And remember, this includes paper, printing, production and postage costs. A remarkable deal! Just think at 37cents the postage alone would cost you $74.00. Here you get everything for only $100.20!

Take another example – a four-page full-color booklet about your business and services. You want to create and send 200 of these. Production costs would be $559.79 and postage, $60.80 bringing the total to $620.59. Not a bad deal for 200 professional-looking marketing booklets.

Let's just take one more example – a postcard. If you want to create and send a standard black-and-white postcard through USPS, you can pull it off for just $.23 per card! It breaks down to an unbeatable $.04 production cost per card and $.19 for postage. That is an amazing deal.

There are a number of other options available using the USPS Online Mailing service, such as different binding preferences for booklets, full color vs. black/white, glossy or standard for postcards and flyers. The online site also links you to related non-USPS direct mail services in order to meet varied direct mail needs. To find out more about their services and options call your local post office or check out: www.usps.gov

GETTING FREE PUBLICITY

Sending a press release is one of the most effective ways of getting free publicity!

13

Editors are looking for good human interest stories to bring to their readers. Send out press releases on your business. Think like big business and promote, promote, promote. The whole idea behind promotion is to gain maximum benefit from your efforts with minimum expenditure. Keep your mind open to new opportunities to attract clients and market your business, and free publicity is an excellent choice.

If you are giving a fashion show for a club or organization this would be a prime opportunity to get free publicity. Some clubs are so prominent that they garner attention just by the nature of who they are. If you happen to be affiliated with this type of organization and are giving a fashion show, don't pass up the opportunity to get free publicity by sending a press news release to your local newspaper.

Don't forget to contact the guest coordinators at bookstores. They love bringing talented individuals to their audiences. They support the arts. Two opportunities exist with them: If you have a book you can do a signing. Second, they will bring you in for a demonstration on a sewing technique and tie in to promoting other sewing books they have to sell.

Also, the library will be a big help in promoting you. They will get behind you and make the community-at-large aware of what you are doing. They will also send out press releases for you. Follow the marketing model and set up an interview to let the head librarian know about your sewing business.

Also, send press releases to local newspapers about any workshops, classes, seminars, etc. that you are involved in. And above all, let your local congressperson know what you have to offer right there in their district.

Send a press release to the White House to let them know of your business or workshops. Focus on the lack of funding in the budget for home economics and the need for them to get behind a programs or business such as yours to ensure that the industry stays healthy. Don't be shocked when you get results.

Get a list of magazines that pertain to your field of specialty. Let's say that you specialize in home décor. Look at how to tie in what you do with a department of their magazine. Write something that shows you know what you are doing and send a press release.

Use all those vendors to solicit your press release to as well. You will never know how much free publicity and other perks will be afforded you until you step out there. Just be in position to take advantage of it when it comes.

Should you hire an agent, or find someone else to help you at a reasonable cost? If you are creative and come up with a number of ways and contacts to get free publicity, don't forgo the opportunity. Just find someone to help send out the press releases. Get someone with excellent skills and an appreciation of the sewing industry. They don't have to sew, but should at least have respect for what you do. Take time to explain to them what you do so they can better position you in both markets. One of my colleagues found someone to assist her with press releases. The person she found had promoted entertainers with her ex-husband. She was talented in promotions, but did not know much about the sewing industry. So all my friend did was take the time to tell her all about her business and the sewing industry. The lady took the ball and ran with it. It was well worth her invested time and efforts.

You want to make as many businesses, organizations and people aware of your offerings as possible, and a press release garners free publicity. A sample press release appears on the next page.

PRESS RELEASE

Contact for editorial information:
Kay Mead
Public Relations Director
Collins Publications
909-590-2471

FOR IMMEDIATE RELEASE

New Sewing Directory Offers Dual Benefits for Professionals

Chino Hills, California, September 22, 2003 - Collins Publications has announced the arrival of **The Directory of Sewing Professionals**. It is a cooperative advertising campaign for those who wish to put their business cards in a specially designated book appropriately called, *The Directory of Sewing Professionals.* The directory is especially appealing because it is not a standard list of names and addresses of proprietors, but comprises business cards describing (through graphics and design) the type of sewing each professional does, along with the general information such as name, address phone number, e-mail and web site. For those who do not have a business card, Collins Publications will design one for a nominal fee.

The directory will be an elite and sophisticated advertising resource mailed to households and businesses across the United States and Canada. Many serious entrepreneurs focus on one corner of the market, and become highly trained and perfected in the intricacies of that part of the field. For example, some experts specialize in draperies, where others find their niche in sewing for children. The logical course is to have a directory, where consumers can locate a sewing professional of their choice.

It will also serve as the common thread for members to share and network to create success. Members will have a special place on Collins Publications' web site to meet and get acquainted with each other.

For further sales information, please contact Collins Publications, 3233 Grand Avenue, Suite N-294, Chino Hills, CA 91709, 1-800-795-8999.

Please forward all editorial inquiries to Nancy Kay Mead, Public Relations Director, Collins Publications, 1-909-590-2471.

###

BRIDAL AND SPECIAL OCCASION

Over the last several years the bridal and special occasion market has experienced a significant increase in sewing professionals entering the field.

14

Special Occasion

Cruises are the rage these days. Many people would rather take a cruise than fly. Cruise lines offer a unique affair called the Captain's Ball. It's where the Captain gets the opportunity to meet and greet the passengers. It generally starts with a cocktail party where you take pictures and have champagne and hors d'oeuvres. The Captain and his staff welcome you in a receiving line similar to that of a wedding party. Later, depending on which seating you are assigned, you will be treated to a formal sit-down dinner with more celebration featuring the waiters singing or doing some kind of special skit. To attend all of this you are to come in your finest attire. Men usually dress in tux or an elegant suit and tie and the ladies in their after-five or full-length formal gowns. Some even pull out all the stops and wear their furs. On the more sophisticated cruise ships it's a sight to behold.

Marketing to Travel Agents

For the sewing professional who is skilled at sewing wedding or special occasion this is a chance of a lifetime. If you know how to market your business properly, have a keen understanding of the art of marketing, networking and how to participate in co-op advertising (with in-kind businesses), you can enjoy enormous success.

How does this benefit you as a sewing professional?

You can put together a flyer and have the travel agent include it into their mailing to their cruise customers. In certain situations you can pool your resources and do what is called co-operative advertising through direct mail or e-mail marketing campaigns. Or, you can simply exchange client lists.

Special Occasion – Marketing to Travel Agents

Step One:

The first step would be to identify as many travel agents as you can. Make sure they have a strong emphasis in cruise lines. Find out how many cruise ships they have actually been on. Most agents get to travel free or for next to nothing so that they can experience what it's like. This way they can better sell the product to their customers. In addition, as it relates to your business, they have a better idea of what would be required for the Captain's Ball. Consequently, they can better appreciate the need for your services. Once you have established which agents are appropriate for targeting, it's time to draft a letter introducing yourself and your services briefly. I say briefly because you will go into detail in your face-to-face meeting with them later.

In your letter you would follow our standard format of keeping it to one page. Tell the agent you will follow-up with a phone call within seven business days to set the appointment. Make sure you stipulate you only want 15 minutes of their time. Most people do not mind sparing 15 minutes to meet with you. You will clearly state your purpose and the benefits to them.

How to find travel agents:
1. Use the Yellow Pages
2. Use the Internet and search with the following keywords: Travel Agents, Cruise Consultants, Cruises, etc.

How to write the letter:
1. Open with the introduction of you and your business.
   a. Special Occasion -- Ball Gowns
   b. Mother-of-the-Bride
   c. Weddings (remember brides take honeymoon cruises)
2. State a fact that demonstrates you understand their business.
   a. You've attended the Captain's Ball.
   b. You have clients that have attended the Captain's Ball and you've made their gowns.
   c. State the difficulty of finding attire in ready-to-wear (shows demand for you).
3. Go directly to the benefits for them.
   a. Open with the sizzle: Tell them you have brides and other customers whom you can refer to them. (Use as a carrot)
   b. Create the demand to meet with you by stating you have additional benefits you would like to discuss with them in a face-to-face meeting.
4. Tell them you only desire 15 minutes.
5. Tell them you will call in 7 business days to set up the meeting.
6. Close with enthusiasm and demand for you.
   a. "I look forward to meeting with you to explore how we may be of mutual benefit to each other."
   b. "I look forward to meeting with you to share how I can be of benefit to your business."

Step Two:

The phone call is made usually around a time that most business people are receptive to entertaining calls. I have found that between 9 am and 10 am work best for me. Generally people have arrived, had a chance to get their morning coffee and are in the frame of mind to take care of business. As a rule, most people expect calls during that time. Never call a new prospect at 8 am, 12 noon, or after 3 pm. Those seem to be shutdown modes for most individuals and for obvious reasons: At eight in the morning most people are just walking in the door and the sound of someone on the other end of a phone before they have had a chance to settle in is annoying. Likewise, for the noon hour they are focusing on taking their lunch break and their concentration is next to none. At three in the afternoon they are wrapping up loose ends, closing out their day and planning for tomorrow. So be mindful of the optimum calling times and use them wisely. After all, you want the person on the other end to be receptive to your call.

Once you have them on the line, don't beat around the bush. Get straight to the point. Remember, this is not a cold call. You have already gotten your foot in the door by the letter you sent. This is your leverage so use it wisely. Introduce yourself with your name followed by the name of your business. Refresh their memory by saying you promised to call to set an appointment for only 15 minutes to meet with them. Be sure to capitalize on the fact that both of you have in common the same customer, and that this is why it would be beneficial for the two of you to meet. Keep in mind that most people are asking themselves *What's in it for me?* Don't leave them to guess—tell them. Once you have set the appointment, don't forget to let them know that you are enthusiastic about meeting with them. You can convey enthusiasm without sounding phony or overly anxious. Example: "I look forward to meeting with you next Wednesday at ten." Always restate the meeting date and time before you close. It helps them to focus on what they have just committed to. Don't make idle conversation after that. It's time to bring the phone conversation to a close. Plus, it makes you look professional and someone who is adept at taking care of business.

First impressions are crucial; so don't diminish yours by overstaying your welcome. If you can't state your purpose in a timely manner and you tend to babble on, chances are you will not have the capability to keep a face-to-face interview within the time limit you requested. So don't blow it by letting nervous tension overtake you. Rehearse your presentation the night before you call. You will find that rehearsing is an excellent antidote for getting rid of nervous tension.

Tips for making the phone call:
Rehearse the night before. During the call introduce you and your company. Refresh their memory by referring to the letter you sent. Restate the reason for the call. Go directly to the benefits. Remind them you only want 15 minutes of their time. Close with enthusiasm and restate meeting date and time. Be sure to mark your day planner and three-month calendar.

Step Three:

The meeting is where you shine. Chances are the travel agent has never considered the benefit of working with a sewing professional. It's your job to introduce the concept and give it merit as it relates to them. Remember you already know what you want and how the relationship between the two of you will be profitable for both parties. Be mindful of the fact that you must convey these benefits, and you will execute your presentation with clarity and purpose. There is nothing more frustrating for someone than to have their time wasted because you cannot accurately explain why you feel it is important for them to do business with you. Be sure to relay your awareness of the needs of *their* customers with respect to elegant gowns and evening attire; especially for the cruise and more specifically, the Captain's Ball. Tell them (while showing them your designs) you have an excellent line that would meet the needs of their customers. As you see them become more excited about your garments, entertain their comments. Once they have an appreciation for your knowledge and expertise, it is now time to explain to them how you envision the two of you being a benefit to each other. You would start by covering the following points:

How putting together a flyer that can be included in mailings to their cruise customers works. Explain how the two of you can pool your resources and do co-operative advertising through direct mail or e-mail marketing campaigns. Tell them that because you both have in common the same customers, you would be happy to exchange client lists. And don't forget to leave room for them to participate by saying, "I am also open to any suggestions you might have."

After establishing what they feel would work best for them, initiate a start date to make it all happen. If it is a flyer, tell them you will start on the initial draft right away. Ask for their input after you have put something together. Bear in mind, we are still under a 15-minute deadline. If you sense they are raring to go, immediately tell them you wouldn't mind extending the time so that the two of you could rough out a sketch. The idea is to always keep their time in mind. It shows you are truly a professional, which gives them the confidence needed to turn their customers over to you. After all, they have worked hard to get these customers and they don't want to refer just anybody to them.

When you close, do so with a follow-up time and date. It may be to show the initial sketch for the flyer. Or, it may be to come together for a focus meeting to move forward on your agreement. No matter the purpose, it's your job to take charge and move things along. Never, ever forget to thank them for their time.

1. Rehearse the day before.
2. Take your business cards, flyers, portfolio, and sample pieces.
3. Make your presentation with clarity and purpose
4. Show samples and portfolio as you talk.
5. Enlist their comments as they show enthusiasm.
6. Tell them your plan of action.
   a. Direct Mail   b. E-mail Marketing
   c. Co-op Advertising   d. Customer List Exchange

7. Convey the benefits.
8. Leave room for them to make suggestions.
9. Initiate the first effort to provide a concept or sketch, etc.
10. Acknowledge the time. (If the meeting is running past 15 minutes)
11. Make the appointment for the follow-up or focus meeting.
12. Thank them for their time.

In the above model, think of other angles to use with travel agents to get business. Make a list of those that come to your mind. Below are just a few, complete with buzzwords (italicized) for your ad.

1. Bahamas: husband and wife, or family, want *matching outfits*.
2. Don't have *appropriate* summer outfits that are *easy to care for.*
3. *Mothers and daughter* want to *look alike* for the cruise.

Resources for Travel Agents: See Resource Guide in the appendix.

Bridal

As a business consultant, I have had the pleasure of working with a number of sewing professionals. One client in particular stands out in my mind. She owned a bridal salon and wanted to increase her profit margin by a certain percentage. She actually wants to open a new location. When I asked why, she told me she wanted to increase her profit margin by 50% and felt a new location was the only way to do it. I explained to her that opening a new location is a costly venture, much like starting a business from scratch.

I told her I could accomplish the goal of increasing her profit margin by 50% without her opening another location; thus eliminating the costly overhead involved in such an undertaking. She reluctantly agreed and said she would be open to the new idea only if I could assure her of a 50% increase within the first year. I told her if she did not achieve her goal by the close of the first year, I would be willing to reimburse her 25% of my consulting fee. In all my years as a consultant I had never made such an offer. I was that sure it would work.

When she hired me she had never heard of the concept of *in-kind* businesses. This kind of marketing can help to raise profit levels significanly if you develop a healthy working relationship with the owners.
Consumers are very busy people and they prefer to shop where they can acquire a number of products and services all at once. It saves time, money and stress. They like the idea of a one-stop shopping experience. It's evident by the business mix you see in today's society. You go to your grocery store and

you have a number of services available to you: one-hour photo, Starbuck's Coffee Bars, pharmacy, cleaners and a bank. It is unbelievable what is offered just at a grocery store. One day in the future I expect to go there to have my teeth cleaned! Don't laugh, you never know.

In the case of my client, she made items for the bride, bridesmaids, and mother-of-bride, etc. However, she didn't offer much in the way of other products. I spent one afternoon reviewing how she ran her business. I needed to make sure there were no other concerns in the way she operated her business that would cause problems. Aside from a few marketing and minor bookkeeping issues, she was okay. I helped get her set up with a new marketing strategy for her current business structure and had an associate of mine restructure her and computerize her internal records. After she got used to the software she was very happy. Some people are just plain scared of computers.

During my visit I jotted down everything she offered in the way of goods and services. Her shop was beautifully appointed; she clearly had good taste. Her work was to die for, and I was proud to work for her. She paid attention to details and her staff was warm and friendly. The customers seemed to love shopping there. She played soft classical music in the afternoons and jazz in the early mornings. I never did quite understand the psychology behind that; but it worked and that is all that matters. About a year later she finally told me she needed an uptempo beat in the morning to get her motor running. I really loved her sense of humor. Anyway, I had a good enough grasp on her and her business offerings to start developing a plan of action.

I studied the center she was in for possible businesses that would be of help to hers. There was an anchor tenant that did lots of advertising, Sav-On to be exact. She did benefit from the trickle-down effect of the additional foot traffic, but I was looking for something more specific to her customer profile. So that left me to examine businesses within a 5-mile radius of her bridal salon. When I'm working with a client I want them to benefit from my knowledge, so I engaged her in making a list of all the businesses within that radius that catered to weddings, brides and the bridal party. I told her to make sure that they were businesses she liked and had the same aesthetic environment and business principles she valued.

She compiled her list and I had mine; we both had many of the same businesses. I selected one business in each category that fit the image and business ethics of my client and I took the following week to draft letters to each business following the marketing model in this text. I met with several of the businesses on my own before bringing her to meet with them. I wanted to get a feel for how open and receptive they would be to what I had planned before bringing her along and having her disappointed if things didn't work out with a business she admired. I saved two or three contact meetings for her to sit in on and observe the proposal process.

The week prior to the meetings, I told her exactly what I had planned. When I laid out the plan in detail she was really pleased. I showed her some sales projections I had made based upon my findings. The week of the last two meetings I trained her on how to present a proposal to a prospective client.

This was my plan of action: I wanted to turn her bridal salon into a one-stop shopping experience for the whole bridal party by bringing into her business cakes, invitations, photography, florist, limousine service, and tuxedo rental. I explained to her that later we would add other services as she became comfortable working with referral contracts. She loved the idea and did quite well in presenting herself during the remainder of the meetings. I did not have her do any negotiating of contracts. However, I did share my style of negotiating so she could understand how and why I presented contracts for negotiation.

We were extremely successful in getting the businesses she liked to come on board. They could readily see (especially after they visited her salon) the benefit in doing business with her. I designed special referral forms for the orders she would take in the salon and we had a new stamp made to place her information on the backs of all the participating businesses' marketing materials or cards. On the contracts I set the start dates all the same so we could have every new service in place for the new grand opening. I'll explain the grand opening later.

We gave ourselves 30 days to rearrange the salon. It was easy and very inexpensive. Only one structural change was made to provide space for a small display of tuxedos. She placed the printer's album of invitation samples and his business cards along with the limousine brochures on a table draped with a lace tablecloth. On a nearby table we had a beautiful display of a cake and flowers from the bakery and florist along with their albums and marketing materials. One of the nicer features was the courtesy pictures taken by the photographer. Now gracing the walls were pictures of bridal gowns made by my client. The photographer's business cards were mounted below each picture on gold-leaf card stock. She placed three of his photo albums on the tables in her waiting area along with his cards. It was a beautiful salon and every business involved was proud to be a part of it.

Now about the grand opening; it was one of the nicest events I'd had the pleasure of working on in a long time. Every one of the businesses contributed and made this more than what any of us had expected. Press releases were sent out and she used local students to meet and greet guests. The grand opening was a huge success.

I made good on my promise to my client. Within the first quarter of implementation of her new goods and services she increased her profit margin by 50%. She is quick to tell anyone that this kind of marketing does pay off. She has since increased her services; she has a new system of checks and balances that has made it easy for her to keep track of referral sales. This form of marketing works for any business whose owner is willing to put it to the test!

Sample Post Card and Flyer for a Bridal Business

The Formal Man

Specializing in fine attire and alterations for men
Zachary Wingate
2000 Windsor Lane ▼ New York, NY 10010
1-555-555-5555

SPRING SALE!

Saundra's Bridal

Full Service Creations
&
Alterations

For a limited time:

Save 30% on any custom-made dress
Save 20% on alterations
Save 15% on all accessories

Call now for an appointment!

Saundra's Bridal
123 Anyroad Suite A
Some City, CA 91709
800-555-5555

CUSTOM TAILORING

Women have a new take-control attitude with regard to wardrobe and home purchases. They are sophisticated shoppers who value their individuality and prefer to have their clothing custom tailored.

15

When I decided to focus on custom tailoring, I too had to profile my customer. Being a woman, I had a pretty good idea of some of the buying patterns and mode of thinking. However, as an entrepreneur I left nothing to chance—I did my homework!

Profile of my customer

Billions of dollars are spent each year by consumers to stay abreast of the latest in fashion, whether it is buying ready-to-wear for them or their family, from major department and specialty stores or decorating their homes. Women all over the world share a common bond...the love of fashion. Every aspect of their lives must be fashionable. Fashion quietly makes a statement about you, and your status in life. The first impression you receive regarding an individual comes from their outward appearance or the aesthetics of their home. Women are simply fascinated with fashion.

They have a new take control attitude regarding decision making concerning their wardrobe, family and home purchases. These women are sophisticated shoppers and value their individuality. For this reason, a number of fashion forward women choose to lead rather than follow by having their clothing custom made, for both themselves and their families. Not to mention the fact that they think nothing of having the interior of their homes artfully done by one of the sewing professionals specializing in home decor. They want to control the decisions over fit, style, color and fabrication. They are part of an undying breed of women who uphold the saying "Born to Shop". Understanding these key elements about my customer's personality allowed me to enjoy enormous success.

Exercise: Pick out the key facts about this customer. *See answers at the end of this chapter.*

Billions of dollars are spent each year by consumers to stay abreast of the latest in fashion, whether it is buying ready-to-wear for themselves or their families, or decorating their homes. Women all over the world share a common bond...the love of fashion, every aspect of their lives must be fashionable. Fashion quietly makes a statement about you, and your status in life. The first impression you get regarding an individual comes from their outward appearance or the aesthetics of their home.

Women have a new take-control attitude with regard to decisions about wardrobe, family and home purchases. These women are sophisticated shoppers and value their individuality. For this reason, a number of fashion-forward women choose to lead rather than follow by having their clothing custom made, for both themselves and their families. They think nothing of having the interior of their homes artfully done by one of the sewing professionals specializing in home décor. They want to control the decisions over fit, style, color and fabrication. They are part of an undying breed of women who uphold the expression "Born to Shop".

Understanding these key elements about my customer's personality has allowed me to enjoy enormous success.

My marketing approach

"Why Custom Tailored Clothing." We're going to take a look at a marketing tool I put together some time ago for my business. It takes advantage of a technique called subliminal advertising. We are all exposed to this on a daily basis as we sit in front of the television or listen to the radio. Advertisers are getting their messages through to the ultimate consumer in a very subtle and effective way. We are constantly influenced through subliminal advertisement. There is no reason why it can't work for your business.

With this type of advertisement there is a lot being said. To avoid discounting your message you must choose a way to capture the client's attention and inform them while doing so. If you can arouse their curiosity, chances are they will read the entire flyer. The good news is even if they do not, they'll still get the message through the bold captions if you design it properly.

If you look at the form, at first glance it looks awfully wordy. You might think, *Who in the world is going to read this?* You'd be surprised. If you'll follow along you'll see that the form has a step-by-step progression to lead the reader through the message. The bold print of this form utilizes subliminal advertising effectively as a marketing tool. The reader can get the message without ever reading the whole flyer.

Dissect Form: Follow the form as the bold captions are explained, you will begin to see the logic. Let's walk through the form to understand each step. See example on the next page for reference.

The "Why Custom Tailored Clothing" is a subliminal advertisement piece that is used in a variety of ways. Occasionally it is used as a direct mail piece. It is always given to the client during the clerical phase of the initial interview, along with the business policy. Remember you must inform your clients. And this piece validates why your services are valuable.

The form's heading asks the lead question: *Why Custom Tailored Clothing?* You'll note in the first paragraph in bold print you'll see the word "fit" which immediately answers the question *Why to Custom Tailored Clothing?* (For fit) In the second paragraph it says no fit, no wear. Now some of us know we may be a size 10 but we buy a size 8; wear it once out of a sense of guilt, and it

Sample Text for "Why Custom Tailored Clothing" Flyer

WHY CUSTOM TAILORED CLOTHING?

Create a wonderful wardrobe by having your clothing custom tailored. Don't let the department stores dictate your since of style. By having clothing custom tailored, you select the style, color, and fabrication...and get the proper FIT!

So often, we feel obligated to purchase clothing that simply does not fit. It is either too large or too small, too short or too long! Thus, creating a purchase that gets worn once, maybe twice, and ultimately lost in our closet forever. "NO-FIT-NO-WEAR". Sure, we wear it once out of guilt, after that we feel justified in forgetting we ever purchased it!

There are a number of benefits derived from having your clothing custom tailored. Clothing is personalized for your particular body type....your personal style....color and fabrication. It allows you to be in total control.

My clients have become so particular that they simply refuse to allow department stores to have control over wardrobe decisions. THEY CHOOSE TO HAVE THEIR CLOTHING CUSTOM TAILORED.

If you have a strong desire to control your fashion statement, but feel insecure due to lack of knowledge regarding proper style for your particular body type, or the appropriate color or fabrication, I CAN HELP! I meet with my clients in the privacy of my office and sewing studio, where all decisions are made in a comfortable, and relaxing environment. Through my knowledge and expertise, I can assist you in making those delicate decisions. Wardrobe consultation can be extremely beneficial and fun. Before "YOU" know it, you will be an expert!

I carry a wide selection of pattern catalogs, such as McCall's, Simplicity, New Look, Style, Vogue, Butterick and Burda, or we can custom design an outfit to your specification.

I WELCOME THE OPPORTUNITY TO TALK WITH YOU. For your convenience I have available "My Business Policy." For further information or to schedule an appointment, you may contact me, BARBARA WRIGHT SIKES, at 714-464-0078.

winds up in our closet—never to be seen ever again. So many consumers in my business have that same problem and I recognized there was a need for my services based on this. Remember going back to the needs of the ultimate consumer and creating demand. In the second paragraph, "no fit, no wear" reminds them of the consequences of clothing that fits poorly.

Then we come down to the fourth paragraph. I call this paragraph my curiosity, or carrot, line. It says, "They choose to have their clothing custom tailored." Keep in mind, they are wondering who else has these concerns and how did they solve them. By this time I'm drawing the interest level of the reader to pursue the bold print for answers to a universal problem. The next paragraph reads just like a sentence as I say to them, "I can help." This sets the stage to validate my value to the reader. What am I helping them with? Remember that fitting problem in the first paragraph. I can help them with their fitting problems. Then the word "you" emphasized they are the ones who now need my help to solve their problem. In the last paragraph is where you see what I call my welcome mat. It says. "I welcome the opportunity to talk with you." And how to you contact me? "Barbara Wright Sykes" and my phone number, "714-590-2471."

Examine the abbreviated text below and see the organization of the bold text that leads the reader to the conclusion—a call to action. I ask for the business in the close.

At the top of the form it asks the question, "**Why Custom Tailored Clothing?**" The next bold caption says "**Fit,**" which answers the question. The following caption drives the point home "**No-Fit-No-Wear**". The next phrase was designed to arouse the curiosity regarding who: "**They Choose To Have Their Clothing Custom Tailored.**" From there it flows in a series of direct statements: "**I Can Help!**" "**You**" "**I Welcome The Opportunity To Talk With You**" and finally it brings them to the contact line, "**Barbara Wright Sykes**" "**714-590-2471.**"

Develop a tool for your business that utilizes the subliminal approach to convey your marketing message.

ANSWERS TO EXERCISE

Women all over the world share a common bond...the **love of fashion**, every aspect of their lives must be fashionable. Fashion quietly makes a statement about you, and your status in life. The first impression you get regarding an individual comes from their outward appearance or the aesthetics of their home.

Women have a new take-**control** attitude with regard to decisions about wardrobe, family and home purchases. These women are **sophisticated** shoppers and **value** their **individuality**. For this reason, a number of **fashion-forward** women choose to **lead** rather than follow by having their clothing **custom made**, for both themselves and their families. They think nothing of having the interior of their homes artfully done by one of the sewing professionals specializing in home décor. They want to control the decisions over **fit**, **style**, **color** and **fabrication**. They are part of an undying breed of women who uphold the expression "**Born to Shop**".

Key Words

Love of fashion	Sophisticated	Value individuality
Lead (leader)	Custom made	Born to Shop
Control	Fashion Forward	Fit
Style	Color	Fabrication

16

Your portfolio should have ample pictures of babies and children wearing your designs. These visuals work well to lure parents and family members to do business with you.

Babies Make Good Business

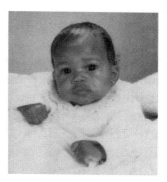

Sewing for babies has been increasing in popularity. It's not uncommon for parents or grandparents to want to see their little darlings in something special, or to have their nursery done in the latest motifs. That's where the savvy sewing professional who can offer those services will prosper. This is the ideal time to gear up and send out your flyers or brochures to your current stable of clients or buy a list of mothers-to-be or homeowners with children and go for it!

Take a visit to your local baby store for inspiration. Look at what they are offering the parents. Most specialty stores like Babies 'R' Us and others, have beautiful clothing for both infant boys and girls. With the forward thinking of modern parents you have a wide range of color combinations and styles to present. They like a bit of whimsy for their babies. Create characters that are special and can be your signature. And give your line instant name recognition and brand awareness. Think of a concept you can capitalize on and put it on all of your ad pieces. Take a picture of one of your clients' cute babies in one of your creations and use it to lure parents to your line.

Contact the major parenting magazines and send them a press release when you come out with new offerings. Write an article on your line; make it easy for them to publish an article on you. Send lot of pictures of babies in your clothing. Get your testimonials from past customers and put them in a media kit.

Get your phone book and locate as many baby stores as possible and show them your line. Do the same for maternity stores. Team up with one of your peers and make matching outfits for mother and baby. I recall seeing a beautiful matching robe set for the new mother and baby when my daughter was expecting. There are some independent entrepreneurs that have stores catering to mom-to-be and infants. Solicit them to carry your line. Design something you can give them an exclusive on; perhaps a special color or fabric you'll use only for their orders, and sell them on the idea. Most of them belong to various organizations that cater to your customer. Ask them for referrals.

Of course you will use the marketing model to plan your campaign. Keep thinking of the ways in which you can get your name out and your line represented. Don't forget to send press releases to Gerber, Beech-Nut, Johnson's and any other business that has the same customer in common with yours.

Layettes – Decorating Baby's Room

Here's another marvelous opportunity to sell your items. If you specialize in baby layettes, contact the companies I mentioned previously and follow that lead. Send interior designers your catalog or flyers. They come in contact with many new parents and parents-to-be. If they have a showroom, get them to let you put out a display. Do not overlook the maternity shops. Most furniture stores don't carry baby cribs, but some do. Do your homework and find them. The layette would do well for you on display in the baby furniture section of a specialty store. However, it should include bumper pads and other items associated with the baby's room.

If you haven't already seen *Nursery Décor*, you should take a look at this book. There is a bevy of great ideas for a baby's nursery. Never before have I seen a book dedicated to this specialty. Author Debra Quartermain expertly guides readers through creating four special themes for baby's room décor: "The Enchanted Garden," "Boys, Bears, & Baseball," "Sail on a Sea of Stars," and "*B* is for Baby." Using felt and fabrics, readers are shown how to create 40 different accessories to fill the themed nurseries, including pillows, toys, stuffed animals, blankets, mobiles, frames, bookends, a toy box, and a rug. Painting tips and ideas for window treatments are also featured. I really like the book because:

1) It has detailed step-by-step instructions.
2) It's perfect for creating a special gift for baby.
3) It's suitable for any skill level.
4) It includes full-size patterns. What a bargain!

In addition to *Nursery Décor*, there are a number of great books on the market related to sewing for babies and children. If you have the ability to sew for babies, be sure to contact the owners or managers of maternity stores, set up an appointment to visit and introduce yourself. Bring your portfolio, business cards, leave your literature, and ask for the business!

Fashion Shows

When you sew for children, you have a number of clients that can influence a buying decision. First, you have the parents, then the grandparents, aunts, uncles, godparents and of course, depending upon the age, you have the child as your potential customer. You can get a lot of mileage out of repeat business from just one family. I've seen it happen where a sewing professional skillfully orchestrated a fashion show at a day care center and had enormous sales from just one family; and went on to book projects to boot! It will require you to present the concept to the owner or manager of the center in a way that it makes good business sense to them. If you meet with objections, don't give up. Keep trying; someone will say "yes." All you need is one successful fashion show to use as leverage to show the others how the concept works. People are creatures of habit and you must educate them on the value of trying new experiences.

If a center is conducting some type of fund-raiser or event, try to tie into that to encourage their participation. You must be clever in your approach. Offer to contribute a percentage of the proceeds to their cause. You will be giving back to the community and Uncle Sam will let you write it off as a tax deduction. Not to mention the business that will be derived from such a venture. Of course the free publicity will be easy to get with an event involving children and charity. If you get more than two bookings for fashion shows and you haven't put one together before, allow yourself at least a month to plan each one, unless you have the full support of staff members or employees. Keep in mind that you will be working with children, and must work around their schedules and that of the parents to ensure maximum participation.

Think of the residual-free advertising you'll get from those proud parents and family members who broadcast that their little darlings are going to be in a fashion show. You will make sure everyone has your marketing materials to make it easy for them to have bragging rights.

Using the marketing model, draft a letter for day care centers. Use your phone directory to locate as many centers as you desire within a given radius of your business. Start your campaign well ahead of the time you wish to conduct the fashion shows. For those who deny you the opportunity, ask them to allow you to place your business cards and brochures at the counter in attractive Lucite stands. Follow up periodically to make sure they have ample supplies in the stands each month. Never leave a prospect without asking for the business. Ask them for referrals of the owners of other day care centers and get permission to use their names as reference.

Keeping a look and feel consistent: I've mentioned keeping the look and feel of your graphics and pieces consistent. I think the two pictures below from the Warm Heart line will help further demonstrate my point. Although each fashion and drawing is different, the style remains consistent. It's from the Jane Ambrose Button line. She is a business consultant specializing in creative product development, production, merchandising, pricing, costing, sales and marketing. She started Warm Heart, a wholesale apparel business, which grew into a national brand name. She recently launched her own pattern line— Warm Heart Patterns, featuring children's coordinated clothing. She's featured in the book *Pricing Without Fear*, if you'd like to learn more about her.

Lemon Kids Case Study

Scenario: A sewing professional specializing in children's clothing must develop an image for her line. She must appeal to children between the ages of two and nine. She had decided, based upon the demographics of her market, that this is the ideal age range for her designs. She must make the following marketing materials: flyer, business cards, stationery and web site. Once she has developed her graphics and color choices it will be easy to transfer them to all mediums.

I put together a case study for one of my seminars on marketing. I used fictitious names and information in the ad to show my audiences how using the assets at your disposal can serve to give you brand awareness. See the ad on the next page.

If you have a unique name, use it to add spice to your image. The name Catherine Lemon was easy to work with. I used the last name "Lemon" for inspiration. I felt it would make it easy for the customers—especially her young ones—to remember. Plus the logo would be recognizable and fun for her little customers.

The design process: I searched my clip art library for lemons. I wanted clip art so I could bring it into Microsoft paint and manipulate the graphic. I found graphic I wanted. Next I decided on the use of primary colors because children gravitate toward them. If you notice, manufacturers make their early toys in those colors. My next step was to find a little boy and girl graphic that was playful and had an elementary feel to it. Once I found the girl, I had the computer search for graphics with the same look and feel. Then I found the little boy in the same line. They were plain line art that needed some additional touches to get the look I was after.

Fonts: Next I needed to find a font that fit something a little child would do. I chose Comic Sans Ms 30 points for the header. The remaining fonts were in the same style with different point sizes.

Clip art: I started with the lemon. I painted the rind lemon yellow, the darker sections were lime green. I added tiny red dots in each of the sections for interest, and made the seed black for contrast. The bar leading from the lemon and the border were lime green with a red line surrounding it. The header text was black.

Next I brought the little girl and boy into my Paint program and made her dress and shoes red and her top blue; the book a deeper shade of green. With the little boy I had more to experiment with. I made his hat, red, lemon yellow and lime

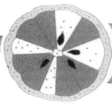

green. His sweater and socks are lime green and his shorts lemon yellow. I originally painted his shoes red, but because of the colorful hat, that made the graphic look unbalanced, so I put stripes on the shoes for a touch of whimsy and painted them red and white. My inspiration came from a candy cane I had seen while looking for Christmas clip art. Due to the white space surrounding each of those graphics I had to add some text for continuity; hence the words *boy* and *girl*.

Chalkboard: I wanted the important company and contact information to stand out. Children are accustomed to chalkboard so I thought that would be nice touch they could identify with. I later added the little heart to bring in some red for contrast. The writing is white on a black background.

Text Image and Branding: I used the lemon name to make the consumer remember the important information:

By: Catherine Lemon   Web site: www.lemon-kids.com
Phone: 909-kid-stop   E-mail: kids@lemon.com

No one's going to forget Lemon Kids' Clothing or how to contact Catherine. This is representative of capitalizing on a theme.

"It was actually easy, plus...I made $500 dollars upholstering the matching chairs...I later sold her on letting me upholster two ottomans for $200 dollars. It was a piece of cake!" Excerpt of letter from Edie, a sewing professional new to the field of home décor.

The Furniture Stores

A furniture store can be a home décor specialist's best friend. Just imagine your designs in the window of a large furniture store or on the showroom floor. It is possible. All you need is to get one client and use them as leverage to get others. But first you must set the stage to make your presentation. As always you will follow the marketing model to prepare your letter and take the necessary steps to setting up the interview.

If you don't already have a portfolio with excellent pictures of your work, you will have to develop one. Make four sample ensembles: King Bedspread, King Comforter, and Daybed. The ensembles should include all the accessories such as neck roll and envelope pillow, plus a variety of pillow shams. Stylize a room using each. Make sure you accessorize with appropriate items. The eye automatically goes to color; use your themes wisely to create interest. Next, you will take several pictures of each. Hire a photographer if you don't feel you can take good pictures.

Once you get your picture into your computer, or you hire a graphics artist to put this together for you, you can manipulate the picture in a photo editing software program. You can make the bedspreads different colors without having to make another sample. There are so many different things you can do to your pictures to show the items come in other colors. Experiment and have fun. Once you have the looks that you want, it's time to assign product codes and place them into your portfolio. Next you will use the design techniques outlined in this book to make your marketing materials. Be sure to stipulate what color ways you can offer each item in as well as the sizes.

Now you are ready to meet with the manager or owner of the furniture store. Make sure you ask for the business. Offer to negotiate the contract. Use the consignment agreement in the forms offered by Collins Publications. If you need further assistance on this process read *Do You Sew For Profit: A Guide for Wholesale, Retail and Consignment.*

When you start to do volume sales you should contract with a fabricator such as Virginia Quilt Inc. at 1-800-757-1856. They specialize in home décor and offer discounts to designers. They can mass produce your orders and allow you to multiply yourself.

Upholstery: When I was on tour I met a young lady (Edie) who was just defining the type of sewing she was going to specialize in. At the time, I don't think she realized the number of professionals in her community with that same idea. As you read her letter on the next page, you'll see why.

Later Edie called Collins Publications looking for me. Unfortunately, I am not at Collins Publications on a daily basis. At any rate, I dropped Edie a note telling her I indeed remembered her and was pleased she thought enough to call and keep me posted on her progress.

Around that same time Collins Publications had started the new home décor section of their catalog and web site. They were carrying a number of new books on the subject. They sent Edie an updated catalog. Edie wrote telling me of her problems regarding her competition. Unfortunately, she was starting to feel like giving up home décor and trying something new. I wrote and encouraged her to try exploring other avenues of home décor that might help her to compete and bring extra revenue. I told her to try upholstering furniture. She wrote and told me of her fears regarding upholstery; she didn't feel that would be something she could be good at. She stated she had seen the books on home décor and there was one on upholstery, but she just wasn't inspired to do upholstery.

I was pleased when I saw Edie once again at one of my seminars. I told her to at least try to upholster something in her home, just to get her feet wet, and see how she liked it. I didn't hear back from Edie for a long time. Then one day I was at a meeting at Collins Publications when I was given a letter from Edie. It's so gratifying to see someone succeed. I will always remember Edie. I hope Edie inspires you to follow her lead and try something you haven't tried before. Explore and see what you can learn to grow your home décor business.

Note: Last month my husband made a bench for the foot of our bed. I used the book *Easy Upholstery* to assist me in upholstering my new bench. I used fabric from two occasional chairs I had professionally upholstered. I was very proud of my accomplishments. Although I don't plan on using those skills in my business, it serves to prove that you can do anything you set your mind to.

Dear Sir:

My name is Edie and I called you to speak to Ms. Wright Sykes some time ago. I saw her at a seminar and I got a letter from her. I just wanted her to know I did follow her advice. I know she's not there but if someone could be kind enough to pass this along to her I would appreciate it.

I live in a city that has a number of nice homes. The majority of them were built in the last five years and the developers are constantly building more each year. In the surrounding area there are a lot of sewing professionals; not many do dressmaking or custom sewing. Most of them do home décor, for the obvious reasons. Needless to say, the competition for business is fierce! I make a decent living at providing these services, now. However, I had never upholstered anything in my life. Matter of fact, I always shied away from it because it looked too difficult for me to even consider.

One afternoon I lost a project to one of my competitors. While having a pity party for myself, it occurred to me what Ms. Wright Sykes had told me. I needed something to set me apart from the pack. I thought; why not add a special service to my business to help me gain more customers in an otherwise overcrowded community of sewing professionals. I had got a catalog from Collins Publications; it wasn't until I read about the book *Easy Upholstery* that it dawned on me I could do it. I ordered the book and started upholstering items for my own home. Boy did I feel good about myself when the compliments started pouring in.

To my surprise, last month I got my first contract for upholstering two chairs. It came from one of my clients who ordered drapes and a bedspread from me. Keep in mind that in the past the subject of upholstery would conjure up fear in me. Was I nervous? You bet I was. I immediately thought about the book *Easy Upholstery*. I reviewed the sections I needed to prepare for the project. After I jumped into the chapter on chairs it took away my fears. What I liked most about this particular job was it was actually easy, plus I had a chance to make extra income by offering my new service. I made an additional $500 dollars upholstering the matching chairs for her bedroom. Oh, by the way, I forgot to mention I later sold her on letting me upholster two ottomans for $200 dollars. It was a piece of cake!

I've changed my business cards and printed new flyers. Not only do I offer home décor, I now specialize in upholstery. Thanks to the book and the fact that I overcame my fear of Upholstery...

Catalog and Web site: With the same pictures you can now have a retail catalog sales business and put them on your web site. Use your fabricator to take the stress off you with respect to hiring employees. Follow the design principles for laying out your catalog and web site marketing each as detailed in this text. See the chapter on "Monitoring Your Progress" to make sure you track profits.

Tip: Call Virginia Quilting and ask for their catalog, add your profit margins to their list and make your catalog using their model, just add your pictures. They even do specialized quilting designs.

Interior Designers: Many AIA members contract out their orders to sewing professionals. Get a list of those in your area and solicit business from them. Work out the percentages and other details of the contract. Have frequent meetings with them in the beginning to ensure you both understand how the relationship is progressing. You don't want to lose the business because of lack of communication. Learn what they need and what is current in the industry. Visit design showrooms in the furniture marts near you. Subscribe to industry magazines and attend trade shows so you can be on the cutting edge of change. Join any organizations that can boost your sales and elevate your awareness of the industry-at-large.

Real Estate Sales: Don't hesitate to pursue this market. Send the letter to the managers of real estate offices using the marketing model. Set the interview date and ask to give a brief presentation to their sales associates and brokers. Most offices have weekly meetings and the majority of the agents are present. This would be an excellent time for your presentation. Take a number of your cards and brochures. For this particular meeting, it would be nice if you had the means to show your pictures on an overhead or some type of projector. Turn your photographs into a medium where they can be seen. Chances are the office manager may have the device needed for your presentation.

While there try to meet and greet as many of the agents as possible. Let them know you would be happy to reciprocate leads. Develop long and prosperous working relationships with as many agents as possible. Periodically check with them to see if you can help to stylize an open house using your items. Make your place cards to put near the bed or perhaps the agent will let you have your brochures available as well. Be present on the day of the open house and answer any questions the visitors have. Be careful not to distract from the purpose of the open house or the agent will be annoyed. Work out all these details ahead of time so you know your boundaries. Make this a win-win experience for all.

Textile Manufacturers: See the information in "Free Marketing Money" and follow those principles to get fabric for your marketing projects. Be sure to give credit to the source on all advertising and promotions pieces. Make sure you find out how much of the fabric is available before you advertise that you can offer it in mass. These details will have been worked out prior to your making the display item for the showroom.

Interior Décor Ad

South Asian Designs

Wong's
Sue

Drapes
Upholstery
Custom Designs

Living room
Dining room
Bedroom

Contemporary Styling with a Middle Eastern Flair

Since 1992

4044 Cornell Canyon Road, Riverdale, AZ 44444
1-555-555-5555

Open 7 Days

Sample Home Decor Ad

DESIGNING A WEB SITE

A web site serves as an additional tool in your arsenal of weapons to gain the attention of the ultimate consumer.

18

There's no getting around it, the Internet is here to stay. Why should you have a presence on the Internet? Hopefully your answer does not hinge on "because everybody has one" but rather because it would be a good marketing tool for *your* business. It serves as an additional tool in your arsenal of weapons to garner the attention of the ultimate consumer and move them to action. Having said that, let's take a look at how to build a good web site for a sewing business—no, make that *any* business. There are several areas we will explore in this chapter: web site design, shopping carts, electronic marketing through e-mail newsletters and affiliate programs.

What kind of site do you want to have? Do you plan to educate as well as offer products for sale? Do you want to have the customer process their sales in what they call real time, online through a shopping cart software program? Or will you forgo that process because you don't have an online merchant account. For more information on setting up an e-commerce merchant account see *The "Business" Of Sewing Volumes 1 and 2.* For now we will discuss both options.

1. Showcase and sell your new items, but not have real-time order processing. Customer will download an order form, fill it out and e-mail or mail it to you.

2. Showcase and sell new items with real-time order processing. Plus, have an e-newsletter complete with links to join.

These will be our two case studies. Before you examine the sample site, please review the checklist on the next page and get acquainted with what's involved in a good site. Then go to the pages that show each of the case studies above. These designs are among a few of many options available to design sites. They are done simply to give you a frame of reference for some of the pages and features that go on certain pages. Can you change and reinvent the wheel? Absolutely. If you find the scope and direction of your content lends itself in a slightly more unique fashion, go for it. However, keep the basic principle of making the site easy to navigate and clearly understandable in terms of what you have to offer. Review the chapter on *Design Elements*; many will apply here as well.

Checklist for designing a web site

A fully functional site should include these crucial pages:
- A home page with your business name
- A contact information and address page
- A product information and pricing page
- A customer service page with product warranty information and return policies

Some additional points to consider when building your web site:

Is the home page clear and compelling?

Is it clear what goods/services you're selling ?

What links will you include on your home page?

Have you included a full product list page?

Will you elaborate each products you sell?

Including links to similar/related items on various individual item info pages.

Have you included several links to shipping charges for items?

Have you included a site map with a link from the home page? (A site map makes the web site easy to navigate.)

Does the site make your customer feel: Sophisticated? Respected?

Included business contact information in relevant places with names, address, phone numbers, fax numbers, departments (customer service, ordering, etc.).

Have you included a page on your privacy policy? This tells what you will, and will, not release about your customers' personal information.

Included a copyright page/note with the appropriate symbol (©).

Have you considered what it is that will make the customer want to return to your site for more business? Perhaps you offer additional services?

Will you have a shopping cart?

Sample Web Site – Home Page

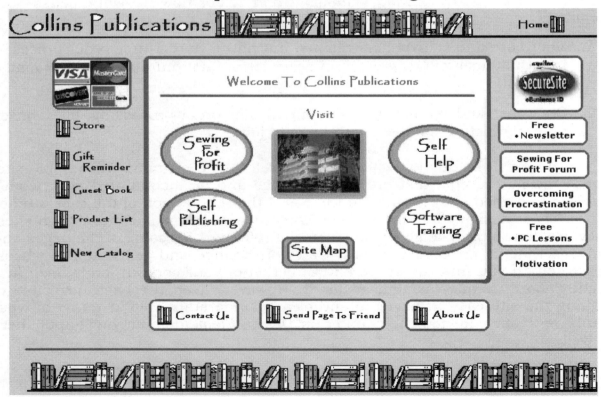

Sample Web Site – Specialty Page

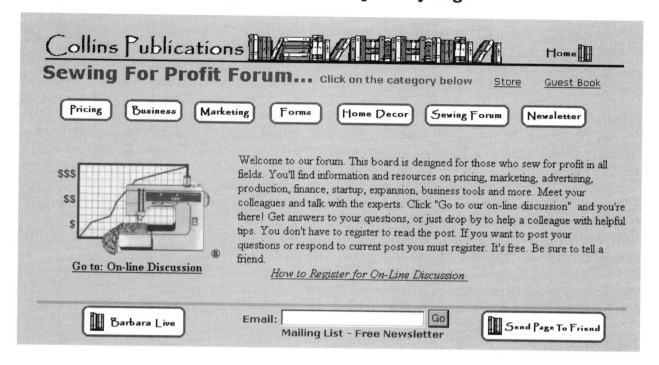

Shopping Cart Example

What is a shopping cart?

A shopping cart enables your customers to select from products your business offers and purchase them on your web site. It's done through a software program with an interface that works like a virtual grocery cart. When customers reach your online shopping cart, they can choose to click on links associated with the product they want and add it to their cart. They can then choose to continue shopping or purchase the item immediately. Items that are selected remain in the shopping cart until purchased or removed. Some software programs have limits on time customers can hold items in their cart without purchasing them. Take a look at other sites. You'll notice some allow you to store items for indefinite periods of time, and will allow you to close your web browser and return at a later time. Certain programs require that you sign up or register before you can purchase, while others give the customer the option. These are features to consider when selecting software programs. Some banks offer shopping cart software when you set up a merchant account with them. Check with your preferred bank to find out what services they offer.

Depending upon the needs of your business, it may be better for you to move beyond a basic Internet shopping cart to a more extensive Website. There are several software programs available to facilitate personal website creation. Some of these are Adobe Page Maker, Microsoft Publisher, and Microsoft Front Page. If you are unfamiliar with HTML programming, the aforementioned programs may become your best friends; they don't require such knowledge.

If you prefer a hands-off approach to designing and maintaining your web site, then certainly outsourcing the project would be ideal. If you decide that hiring an outside webmaster to create your site is more up your alley, remember to consider set up costs. Since a fresh-looking site is a key to a successful online business, inquire about maintenance costs as well.

Affiliate Programs

Affiliate programs are great marketing tools. They are particularly useful—if not vital—for e-commerce businesses since they can greatly enhance your exposure to customers you might not otherwise reach.

If you are unfamiliar with affiliate programs, let me briefly explain. In an affiliate program, you link up with another e-business so they can offer electronic advertisements/links or recommendations to your web site. You will likely pay them a fee for the traffic they send you, although the fee is nearly always based on performance. This means that the more hits to your web site through your affiliate's link, the more effective his/her link probably is (i.e., it is performing well), and they should be compensated in kind. The cleaner your site is and the easier to navigate, the more likely your affiliate will confidently endorse your site, and the more effective your relationship will be. In most cases you will design the ad on their site. Since this will be the first glimpse customers get of your business, you need to ensure that this first impression is as clear and compelling as possible.

Types of Affiliate Programs

There are generally two types of affiliate programs: internal and external. Internal programs mean you take charge of most of the grunt work. You select the copy and essentially manage the program yourself. With no extra commission or overhead fees, internal programs tend to be cheaper than external ones.

External programs will often offer you a lot of services, but can add up in costs since you are paying not only for commissions and overhead, but in many cases set-up and maintenance fees as well. Furthermore, you may benefit from a third party's more objective monitoring capabilities. External programs may also serve you by offering user-friendly interfaces with professional reporting systems of use to both the merchant and the affiliate. In addition, some people feel having a third party involved raises the bar on accountability so that parties are compensated as fairly as possible.

Affiliate Networks

Affiliate networks often have large member bases full of businesses to which your business can be marketed. Link Share and Commission Junction are the two largest affiliate networks with huge member bases, with fees to match ($1,000 + to set up plus hundreds per month to maintain!). These networks are usually utilized by larger companies. There are less costly alternatives, however. Clixgalore is one of them. They charge no set-up fees and charge reasonably for escrow (third party commission fees). Miva Merchant endorses Clixgalore and reports their interface is remarkably user-friendly; their program is effective, and their customer service responsive.

Search Engines

This is similar to the Yellow Pages, only in an electronic version. There are a number of good search engines you should list your site with. Go to AOL or Yahoo! and use the keywords "search engine." Do your homework to decide which ones you wish to invest your time and or money with. Search engines can be beneficial in driving traffic or visitors to your site. Planted in your site will be a series of keywords behind the pages that help search engines direct to your site visitors looking for what you have.

This may be a little technical, but at least you will know the name of what is behind it. The process is called META tags. Search engines have what the industry calls spiders that go out to sites and index them by their META tags, or keywords. There are other ways in which search engines index sites as well.

Link Exchange: Putting your link on another site that has the same customer in common will be beneficial to driving traffic to your site. You should offer to do the same.

Press Release: When you launch your site, don't forget to send a press release to everyone you can think of. See the chapter "Getting Free Publicity."

Electronic Marketing

E-mail Marketing Newsletter and Other Communications:

Constant Contact is a direct e-mail marketing software program that lets you communicate with your current and prospective customers on a regular basis. The format is clean, contemporary, professional looking, and is much less expensive than traditional direct mail marketing programs. It contains lots of great-looking HTML graphics to help you create pages using templates or customize them the way you like. In addition, an e-mail marketing program such as Constant Contact allows you to link your current and prospective customers back to your web site for greater traffic.

Constant Contact helps you build and manage your subscriber database, and gives you the option to create a link on your web site to "Join my mailing list." The program also allows you to track your campaign and view results immediately. Besides creating and e-mailing regular newsletters, you can also use the program's templates to create and send separate, individual announcements, and other promotional materials.

Most everyone has access to the Internet. You can, in real time, send to your clients announcements of your new line or a specific new design. You can use it to e-mail one or all the contacts in your subscriber database. You can even send out invoices if you like. The program has a number of great possibilities for your business.

For more information visit Constant Contact: (www.roving.com). For other e-mail marketing programs use keywords *e-mail marketing* in your search engine.

Sample Newsletter from Constant Contact

TRADE SHOWS

Planning for a trade show is crucial. You are literally running a business away from home.

19

Trade shows can be a wonderful way to introduce a wide audience to you and your goods and services, but picking the right venue is important. You would be surprised at the unusual ways in which you can use trade shows to your benefit. For many years I have traveled with Collins Publications at various trade shows. I have appeared at a number of sewing trade shows as well.

Planning for the show is crucial. You are literally running a business away from home. Putting all the pieces together will make it a success. First is to decide exactly what you want to feature. Then you can move on to researching the appropriate shows to feature your goods and services. Don't overlook trade shows that may yield benefits, but on the surface seem the most unlikely candidates for you. Case in point:

I consulted with a sewing professional who specialized in home décor. I suggested to her that she attend a trade show for the textile industry. I put together a rough sketch of the marketing concept I had in mind. I explained to her we needed a unique slant to her sales materials. There needed to be something to get them to thinking. We posed the question in our lead headline: "Want Every Furniture Store To Showcase Your Fabrics?" Then we simply built the flyer around telling them how she was the answer to that burning question.

Earlier I had developed a marketing campaign for her utilizing furniture stores, so I knew this would work as well. See the chapter "Home Décor." There's a section on furniture stores.

At any rate, representatives from the many major textile manufacturers were stopping by to hear what she had to offer. Later, I helped her put together a proposal to get them to give her free marketing money for a special project she wanted to promote. You can read more on this in the Chapter 11, where we discuss getting free marketing money.

At another convention held for furniture stores, she took the actual product with her and wrote contracts on the spot. She had to educate the entrepreneurs on how to work with her. But that was easy; again, that's discussed in the "Marketing For Home Décor" chapter. She shared a booth with someone, which helped to decrease her expenses. In addition, she had funds from a textile manufacturer whose fabric graced the bed of her display. She took her portfolio and had an actual bed complete with custom bedding from her new line. Her brochures were in color, largely due to the contributions from the textile manufacturer. There were pictures of her line featured in the window of a local furniture store.

Another very ingenious sewing professional attended a Baptist convention and sold a great deal of her children's line there. She had a captive audience of moms and dads, aunts, uncles and grandparents who couldn't get enough of her line. She also booked appointments.

How to Find a Trade Show

Listed are sources to search for upcoming conventions, expos, conferences and tradeshows. You can search by industry, then by the state you are interested in.

The Ultimate Trade Show Resource   www.tsnn.com
Cyber Expo Search   www.cyberexpo.com

Trade Show Display Contacts

Skyline Exhibits
3355 Discovery Road
Eagan, MN 55121
Toll Free Phone: 1-800-328-2725
Phone: 651-234-6000
Fax: 651-234-6571
www.skycorp.com/skyline

Impact Exhibits
2570 Lafayette St.
Santa Clara, CA 95050
1-888-988-2131 or 1-408-988-3088
Fax: 1-408-727-7481
www.impact-displays.com

Budget Trade Show Displays
12600 Stowe Drive, Suite 8
Poway, CA 92064
(888) 323-6995 or 916) 783-7999
Fax: (916) 783-7532
http://www.monsterdisplays.com

Smart Exhibits
1450 Park Court, Suite 4
Chanhassen, MN 55317
1.800.430.6111
Main: 952.470.6111   Fax: 952.470.6113
E-mail inquiries:
info@smartexhibits.com
www.smartexhibits.com

Free Seminars from Skyline

Eye Power!
Profitable Exhibiting
Designing Effective Trade Show Exhibits

Attendees Receive Free Exhibiting Tools!

Free seminar notebook featuring notes
and worksheets on a variety of exhibiting topics
   (available at select seminars only)
Call: 1-888-988-2131

Effective Exhibiting In A Changing Economy
Better Booth Staffing
Creating Effective Promotions
Measuring Your Trade Show Results

75-page - Creating Effective Trade Show Promotions Book
86-page Trade Show Marketing Idea Kit

Layout and Designing Your Booth

Skyline offers services in custom design, construction, set-up and management of trade show and event exhibits from tabletop-sized to island-sized displays. They offer both sale and rental options. Skyline also offers seminars to teach you how to maximize your trade show potential utilizing high quality customized graphics (using a full in-house graphics supply chain) and display design and engineering techniques. They also offer staffing suggestions for those who will run the exhibit show to help maximize quality leads and sales. Enhance your trade shows by attending our free seminars.

How to Prepare for a Trade Show

1. Picking the right venue.
2. Decide what you want to feature.
3. Will you sell or just get leads
4. Determine a budget
5. Select staff if needed
6. Prepare and order sales materials
7. Book travel and other arrangements
8. Design layout of booth
9. Make list of items needed for booth
10. Order any needed items for booth
11. Round up all needed forms
12. Design and print drawing forms
13. Decide on drawing prize
14. Make sure you have enough leads cards
15. Pre-print your Thank You cards
16. Arrange transportation of stock: to and from venue
17. Train booth help
18. Check seller permit, etc
19. Check insurance carrier for needed documentation
20. Make tax chart for that city
21. Make Price List of all products
22. Review any paperwork for show requirements
23. Order needed electricity, phones, etc.
24. Take inventory of supplies on hand
25. Review display items on hand for present condition
26. Refill any needed medication
27. Send Press Release to media
28. Run any ads if necessary
29. Contact businesses of interest in that city
30. And associations/organization
31. Pack in-flight needs: reading materials, snacks, etc.
32. Pack wardrobe
33. Personal needs: nails, hair, etc.
34. If speaking prepare and rehearse speech
35. Have seminar handouts printed
36. Review teaching aids
37. Tell person in charge what to do while you're away
38. Day before travel arrangements
39. Reconfirm pick up from airport
40. Check weather conditions
41. Touch base with booth staff day before
42. Call hotel day before for room number
43. Check balances on all credit cards
44. Make your own list and check it twice
45. Put dates on the Daily Planner and 3 Month calendar
46. Get money for booth, counter, wrappers
47. Credit card displays
48. Make your final checklist and go over it
49. Have Fun!

Trade Show Inventory Report

This form is self-explanatory. However, it serves as a system of checks and balances regarding Collins Publications stock that is taken on the road. Normally the show lasts three days, as evidenced by the word *Date*. The beginning and ending inventory are next to each other because it makes it easy to see the differences at a glance. The name and location of the show is critical for obvious reasons.

Forms Needed

The forms listed below are the ones I use when I am on tour with Collins Publications, or appearing as a speaker. Generally, Collins Publications will have a booth of their own to take advantage of my appearance. I will come to the booth between lectures to meet and greet seminar attendees. These forms are now being offered in the new *Marketing Forms* from Collins Publications.

Forms List

- ☐ Tour Checklist
- ☐ Tax Chart and Price List
- ☐ Trade Show Inventory Report
- ☐ Currency Log

- ☐ Balance Sheet
- ☐ Daily Sales Report
- ☐ Credit Card Report
- ☐ Registration Form
- ☐ Drawing Form

Items to Check Off for Trade Shows

Stapler/Staples/Remover
License Forms
Resale License
Scotch Tape/Double Face
Inventory List
Rubber Bands
Scissors
Steno Pad
Paper Clips
Easels
Baggies
Bank
Receipts
Currency/Coin Inventory Log
Coin Counter/Wrappers
Cash Box
Credit Card Machine /Signs
Credit Card Drafts –
(Visa, MasterCard, American Express)
Money Bag
Sheets
Towel

Overhead/Transparencies
Press Kit
Recorder & Cassette
Camera/Film
Health Magazine
Book Covers
Galley Copy
Vogue, Threads Magazine
Business Cards
Tax forms
Drawing Flyers
Flyers, Catalogs, Brochures
Banner, C-Print, PR Kits
Banner Hooks
Posters
Poster Knife
Booth Instructions
Bowl/Candy
Artificial Flowers
Table skirt
Gold overlay
Travel Tickets
Personal Checklist

MONITORING YOUR PROGRESS

Marketing, advertising and promoting your business is an ongoing process and must be monitored to ensure you are getting a return on your investment.

20

When putting forth a great deal of time, money and energy to develop good marketing campaigns for your sewing business, you must keep tabs on the progress. It is important to keep the business profitable. Code each piece you send out so it will be easy to determine how someone heard about your business. Some companies put an extra digit at the end of the suite number. Others will put a code right on the marketing piece and some will have an extra line to identify a specific ad campaign. Sometimes it is disguised as a division or department of the company. Start looking at advertising pieces you receive; see if you can find the codes.

In the examples below the code shows the fall advertising campaign. The obvious code here is "F203." They mailed out 203 pieces in this particular campaign. Now they can track how the person heard about them and, if they want a quick reference as to how many pieces went out, it's right on the mailer. The code can be anywhere on the mailer as long as it conforms to postal regulations. Some place the code outside the address lines. Others like to include it in their return address line, especially if they have a bounce-back card or reply card, order form, etc. Decide the method of communication you want to receive from your client:

1. Mail back card/order
2. Call you
3. Visit your store
4. Order on the web
5. Other

How you hear back from the client will determine whether the code should go in your address line. If it's a catalog mailing where they will call you, then you will have the opportunity to ask them the code and therefore you can place the code outside the address line.

Coding Examples

Kay's Custom Interiors
2602 Market Street
Suite 399-**F203**
Inglewood, CA 90305

Code **F203**
Kay's Custom Interiors
2602 Market Street
Suite 399
Inglewood, CA 90305

Kay's Custom Interiors
Division: **F-203**
2602 Market Street
Suite 399
Inglewood, CA 90305

Keeping Track Of What Sells

It's good to have the coding system to find out how a customer came to hear about you. However, one way in which you can ensure that your business continues to thrive is to track which items sell and duplicate those efforts. If a number of your clients seem to be leaning toward a certain item, then perhaps you should advertise it more. Make samples and keep them on display in your studio. Put together a marketing piece and send it to prospective customers. Have some type of tallying device so that you can see the numbers of items that are moving in each category of your sales campaign. Also, see if you can spot a demand for a certain color, style or fabrication developing. When you find something that works, use it. This is part of your market analysis. Customers will vote on what they like by their spending patterns. If you are an astute businessperson you will pick up on their desires and use that to benefit your business.

If you find a particular campaign is losing steam, change an element on the ad piece. Start with the headline; change the lead and put it into another color. Monitor the progress. If the percentage of sales volume rises, then perhaps the old ad had saturated your existing database and people recognized, but didn't respond to it. Or, it may be time to purchase a new list and expose these prospects to the original ad that worked so well with your current clients. As in the beginning you will code each mailer and track the sales activity for consumer buying habits and trends. Never become discouraged when placing ads. It is not an exact science; it is indeed a trial and error process. However, there are those basic rules to follow in designing a piece that will give you the advantage over failure.

Keep your businesses healthy. You don't always have to reinvent the wheel. When you develop a successful marketing campaign use it, and keep testing it at all times. Consumers' wants, needs and desires will shift; therefore monitoring your progress is absolutely necessary in order to thrive in business.

Marketing Material Evaluation

1. WHO CREATED THE AD?   WERE YOU PLEASED?

2. WERE YOU PLEASED WITH THE LOOK AND FEEL OF THE AD PIECE?

3. WAS IT DELIVERED ON TIME? IF NOT, WHY NOT?

WERE MATERIALS DELIVERED ON BUDGET? IF NOT, WHY NOT?

DID THE CAMPAIGN TAKE TOO MUCH TIME?

DID IT AFFECT RUNNING YOUR BUSINESS?

NEXT TIME, WOULD YOU?   DO IT YOURSELF: HIRE HELP?

HOW WOULD YOU IMPROVE THE WHOLE PROCESS NEXT TIME?

_____

_____

About the Author

Barbara Wright Sykes is no stranger to success. She has been the host of a popular radio talk show, and the author of *Overcoming Doubt, Fear and Procrastination,* as well as numerous books, audio's, forms and software. Barbara has been a frequent guest on television and radio, making 125 radio appearances in one year alone. Her TV appearances include: KTLA, BET, WGN, ABC, CBS, and Crook and Chase.s. Wright Sykes has been recognized and praised by leading newspapers and magazines such as the Los Angeles Times, Chicago Tribune, Income Opportunity, and Health Magazine.

Barbara had been the recipient of the prestigious *"International Woman of the Year"* award for her contribution in the fields of business and psychology. Receiving this honor ranked Barbara Wright Sykes in the company of such notables as former President Reagan's daughter Maureen Regan, noted attorney Gloria Alred, journalist Linda Ellerbee, actress Mariette Hartley, news anchor Kelly Lang, and actress Renee Taylor of *The Nanny* television show.

Serving as a business consultant for professionals desiring to start, maintain and achieve success, Barbara founded the firm Barbara Wright & Associates in 1979. Barbara has consulted with: California State University, Midwestern State University, Union Bank and Vogue Magazine, among others. As a successful sewing professional, Barbara was commissioned by the fashion industry's noted designers, tailors and sewing professionals to assist them with pricing, market analysis and business expansion. She penned her first business text book, entitled *The "Business" Of Sewing.* In demand as a business consultant, KTLA's popular morning show "Making It" featured Barbara Wright Sykes as one of Southern California's leading speakers, business consultants and authors.

Stimulating a broad wave of discussion, while arming a vast generation of individuals with the tools necessary for a successful personal and professional life, Barbara travels throughout the year lecturing to standing-room only seminars for corporations, colleges, universities and the private sector. She has served as keynote speaker and workshop facilitator for Wells Fargo Bank, Department of Agriculture, Small Business Development Center, and the International Woman's Council, to name a few.

Barbara has a myriad of knowledge and expertise, she formerly taught college in such disciplines as business, psychology and career development, for which she received the Outstanding Instructor Award. She has developed several popular seminars among those are: *Overcoming Doubt, Fear and Procrastination*; *Pricing Without Fear*; *Marketing Your Sewing Business*; *The "Business" Of Sewing*; *Getting Published—From Concept To Consumer*; *The Five Layers of Relationships* and her most requested *"Yes I Can."* Barbara inspires people with her down-to-earth wisdom, as she guides individuals to their life-long goals. Her motto, "Determination Equals Success!" encourages individuals to look forward to the personal and spiritual satisfaction that life has to offer.

Barbara Wright Sykes has been appreciated and recognized for her hard work and dedication to others. Those who know her well, speak highly of her: One of Atlanta's most successful businessmen had this to say about Barbara: *"I have learned much by observing Barbara in action. It is impossible to know her without experiencing a wealth of energy and enthusiasm. If you're going someplace in life, you will want to know Barbara Wright Sykes . She is a winner."*
— S. Barry Hamdani

To schedule an interview, personal appearance, speaking engagement or consultation with Barbara contact: Ann Collins at Voice: 909-590-2471 or Fax: 909-628-9330

ISBN: 0-9717824-0-7

NEW

Do You Sew For Profit $19.95
A Guide For Wholesale, Retail and Consignment
Barbara Wright Sykes

Do you sew for profit and want to take your business to the next level? This book is for you! It skillfully details how to earn income through the use of wholesale, retail and consignment while sewing for profit. It covers all disciplines of sewing from custom tailoring, home décor, bridal, children's, and art-to-wear, just to name a few. Learn how to make the transition from working with clients, to selling your sewn items through wholesale, retail and consignment. The book focuses on the business, marketing and pricing aspects of each field. Barbara shares her secrets, tips, techniques, knowledge and expertise with you. Plus, several sewing professionals will tell you how they became successful utilizing these principles. The book also covers production cost, finding a manufacturer and Sales Rep, leases, store design, merchandising, color, style, fabrication and more. Order your copy today! $19.95

Partial List of Chapters

Retail:
Sewing in a retail world
Home vs. Commercial space
The Location: Finding Yours
Types of Leases
Store Design
Jeff Grant
Merchandising
Retail Pricing
Retail Marketing

Consignment:
Selecting the consignment site
Negotiating with the owner
Spelling out consignment terms
Commission analysis
Color, Style and Fabric
Inventory management
Consignment Pricing
Consignment Marketing

Wholesale:
Market research
Mass production
Cost of good sold
Manufacturing Cost
Building a profitable line
Product and Garment Cost
Wholesale Cost Analysis
How to save on production
Chargebacks and Markdowns
Finding a good Sales Reps
Combining sewing and art
Running a profitable workroom
Turn your sewing into wholesale
Trunk shows
Victoria Woodford Hunter
Wholesale Pricing
Wholesale Marketing
And more!

Featuring

Frances Harder	*Justin Limpus Parish*	*Diana Cavagnaro*	*Pam Damour*
Fashion Business Inc.	***Art To Wear***	***Hats***	***Home Décor***
Building a Profitable Line	Combine Sewing and Art	Sewing Hats For Profit	Profitable workrooms
Wholesale Cost Analysis	Business Tips	Millinery Types	Calculations Examples
Product and Garment Cost	Trunk Shows	Sewing Studio	Business Tips
Pricing and Marketing	Pricing and Marketing	Pricing and Marketing	Pricing and Marketing

About Collins Publications

Since 1991 Collins Publications has been dedicated to helping you achieve your goals through quality products that teach you how to deal with your fears, enhance personal relationships, improve your business, learn computer software, sew for profit, and publish your books. We offer consulting on a wide variety of topics. Our number one goal is to provide you with the tools for success by offering excellent products, outstanding service, and friendly and helpful staff!

Wholesale Information: Call, Fax or email your request to Collins Publications, and we will send our wholesale terms and discounts. Call 909-590-2471

Catalog

$1.00 for Color Catalog ✱ Free Black/White Catalog
Order Your Color Catalog from Collins Publications
Call for the latest catalog: 800-795-8999 or 909-590-2471
We have four divisions at Collins Publications, they are:
Self Help   Sewing For Profit
Self Publishing   Software Training (Free)

Visit our web site at: www.collinspub.com

Sign Up For...

Sewing for Profit Forum ✱ Free E–Newsletter

Free E-Newsletter: Sewing For Profit
1. Go to http://www.collinspub.com
2. Put your email address in.

Join **Collins Publications** mailing list

Email: [   ] Go

Free Newsletter

How To Register For Sewing For Profit Forum
(Online Discussion)

1. Go to http://www.collinspub.com/forums/policy.asp
2. Scroll to the bottom and press the word Agree
3. Put Email address, User Name, Password, Password Again. The rest are optional.
4. Scroll down and press Submit and you are registered.

When you return to the Forum make sure a check mark is in the upper right-hand corner to save your password. Email us if you encounter difficulty and our webmaster will register for you. Just give your email address, user name and password desired.

Bibliography/Books

Marketing
Marketing Outrageously, Spoelstra, Cuban
Streetwise Do-It-Yourself Advertising, Sarah White
E-Marketing, Judy Strauss
Principles of Internet Marketing, Ward Hanson
The Brand Called You, Peter Montoya, Tim Vandehey
Jim Krause
Marketing Management , Philip Kotler
Strategic Brand Management, Kevin Lane Keller
Starting & Running a Successful Newsletter/Magazine, Cheryl Woodard

Layout and Design
Robin Williams Design Workshop, Williams, Tollett
The Complete Manual of Typography, James Felici
Dynamics in Document Design, Karen A. Schriver
 Layout Index: Brochure, Web Design, Poster, Flyer, etc.

Business
Specialty Shop Retailing, Carol L. Schroeder
Inside the Fashion Business, Jarnow, Dickerson
Apparel Manufacturing: Sewn Product Analysis, Ruth E. Glock
How to Start a Clothing Store, Julie Miller
Do You Sew For Profit:: Wholesale/ Retail/Consignment, Barbara Wright Sykes

Business Continued
Marketing Your Sewing Business, Barbara Wright Sykes
The "Business" Of Sewing Vol. 1, Barbara Wright Sykes
The "Business" Of Sewing Vol. 2, Barbara Wright Sykes
The "Business" Of Sewing (Original), Barbara Wright Sykes
Pricing Without Fear, Barbara Wright Sykes

Reference Books
Books In Print, List all current books by subject, title and author.
Directories in Print, List specialized directories.
Encyclopedia of Associations, List names of professional organizations.
Forthcoming Books, Future books scheduled to appear in Books In Print.
Newsletters in Print, List published newsletters
Paperback Books in Print, List paperback books by subject, title and author

Motivational Books/Tapes
Overcoming Doubt, Fear and Procrastination, Barbara Wright Sykes
Loving Yourself First, Linda Coleman-Willis, LC & Associates
How To Become A Winner, Zig Ziglar, Nightingale-Conant Corp.
It's Time For You, Rita Davenport, Phoenix, Arizona
The Power Of Positive Thinking, Dr. Norman Vincent Peale

What's New at Collins Publications

Sewing For Profit System

Books
The "Business" Of Sewing Vol. 1
The "Business" Of Sewing Vol. 2
The "Business" Of Sewing (Original)
Marketing Your Sewing Business: How to Earn a Profit
Do You Sew For Profit: A Guide for Wholesale, Retail and Consignment
Pricing Without Fear
Overcoming Doubt, Fear and Procrastination

▼

Audios
The "Business" Of Sewing
Marketing Your Sewing Business
Take The Fear Out Of Pricing
The "Business" Of Sewing Audio Album
Overcoming Doubt, Fear and Procrastination
*Overcoming Set
* means book included

Forms
Forms On Computer Disk
The Complete Set Of Forms
*Sew Pro Kit "A" (TBOS Original)
*Sew Pro Kit "B" (TBOS Original)
Home Décor/Interior Design
Marketing
Cornice Styles
TBOS = The "Business" Of Sewing

Newsletters Back Issues also available

Resource Guide

MARKETING A BOOK
Borders Books & Music, Area Marketing Manager
1072 Camino Del Rio North, San Diego, CA 92020

Open Horizon - Book Market
www.bookmarket.com

Complete Guide to Book Marketing
Linda Coleman-Willis/ L.C. & Associates
www.lindaspeak.com

PRINTING/PUBLISHING
Spot Color:
Pantone Matching System. www.pantone.com
Agfa's Color Guides, www.agfabooks.com
TruMatch www.trumatch.com

Writing/Editing/Proofreading/Indexing
Gail Taylor, 800-628-4404
www.savvysecretarial.com
gailtay@email.com

GRAPHIC DESIGN/ WEB DESIGN
K-2 GRAPHIX
Kristi Coop, www.k2grphix.com

PHOTOGRAPHER
Captured Moments by Tami
909-260-0272

GRAPHICS
Go Graphics, http://www.gograph.com/
Bridal, www.geocities.com/Paris/4378/clippeople.html
Sewing Graphics, http://www.sewdoll.com/
MS Office, http://dgl.microsoft.com/

E-COMMERCE, SHOPPING CARTS,
www.novainfo.com   www.miva.com
www.valueweb.net   www.paypal.com
www.iongate.com   www.costco.com

EMAIL MARKETING/NEWSLETTER
Constant Contact: www.roving.com

SUPPLIES:
Quill: www.quillcorp.com
Associated Bag Co: www.associatedbag.com
Priority Mail: www.supplies.usps.gov
Online Stamps: www.usps.gov/ibip

BUSINESS CONSULTANT
Barbara Wright & Associates, Barbara Wright Sykes
barbara@collinspub.com

Fabric Swatch Kit, www.clayhunterinc.com
Victoria Woodford Hunter & James Clay

Newsletter Back Issues 8 Issues
The Business Of Sewing Back Issues
800-795-8999
www.collinspub.com

Diana Cavagnaro, 800-474-4287
Millinery Classes, Video: Straw Hat Class
Softops & Ahead Productions
www.aheadproductions.com

Fabricator: Virginia Quilting Inc
434-447-5091, www.virginiaquilting.com

STORE DESIGN
Jeff Grant (ask about his Store Design book)
Trio: 800-454-4844, www.triodisplay.com

TRAVEL AGENTS/CRUISES:
www.astanet.com   www.acta.net
www.nacta.com   www.travel.org/agents.html
www.cruise4.com/CruiseMagazines.html
www.cruise4.com/BrochuresMenu.html
www.hopcott.com/magazines/cruise.html

MAIL ORDER BUSINESS: Shippers:
FedEx: www.FedEx.com
Airborne: www.aiarborne.com
DHL: www.dhl.com   UPS: www.ups.com
US Postal Service: www.usps.gov

Direct Mail Services: 800-344-7779
NetPost Mailing Online
www.usps.com/mailingonlin

FREE BUSINESS CARDS
Vista Print, www.vistaprint.com

GREETING CARDS ONLINE
American Greeting Cards
www.aol-aol.americangreetings.com

SELF-PUBLISHING/FULLFILMENT
Writing Non-Fiction, Dan Poynter
www.parapublishing.com

SOFTWARE & TUTORIALS
LearnKey, 800-865-0165
www.learnkey.com

KeyStone Learning Systems, 1-800-581-9732
www.keystonelearning.com

DDC Training Services, 800-964-6796
www.ddctraining.com

Peach Pit Press
www.peachpit.com

Osborne / McGraw Hill
www.osborne.com

Connie Amaden-Crawford, 928-204-9362
www.fashionpatterns.com
A Guide to Fashion Sewing
The Art of Fashion Draping,
Patternmaking Made Easy

Justine Limpus Parish, 626-441-5324
Book: Drawing the Fashion Body:
Classes: Shibori Pleating & Beyond
Fashion & Costume Drawing
www.home.earthlink.net/~parishjt

Clotilde®
1-800-772-2891
www.clotilde.com

Nancy's Notions®
1-800-833-0690
www.nancysnotions.com

Barbara Brabec's Books
www.barbarabrabec.com
Handmade for Profit, Make It Profitable
Creative Cash. Homemade Money

Pamela Damour, 802- 872-2746
www.pamdamour.com
Videos: Windows 101
Sensational Swags and Jabots
The Perfect Pillow, Pillow Parade

FINDING TRADE SHOWS
The Ultimate Trade Show Resource:
www.tsnn.com

Cyber Expo Search: www.cyberexpo.com

TRADE SHOW DISPLAY CONTACTS
Skyline Exhibits, 3355 Discovery Road
Eagan, MN 55121, 1-800-328-2725
www.skycorp.com/skyline

Impact Exhibits, 1-888-988-2131
2570 Lafayette St.
Santa Clara, CA 95050
www.impact-displays.com

Budget Trade Show Displays
12600 Stowe Drive, Suite 8
Poway, CA 92064, 888-323-6995
http://www.monsterdisplays.com

Smart Exhibits, 800.430.6111
1450 Park Court, Suite 4
Chanhassen, MN 55317
www.smartexhibits.com

DESIGNING YOUR BOOTH
Free Seminars from Skyline
Profitable Exhibiting
Designing Effective Trade Show Exhibits
Creating Effective Promotions
Call: 1-888-988-2131

Frances Harder, 213-892-1669
Book: Fashion For Profit
Fashion Business Incorporated
www.fashionbizinc.org

SEWING FOR PROFIT SYSTEM
Sewing for Profit System
c/o Collins Publications
3233 Grand Avenue Suite N-294-C
Chino Hills, CA 91709
www.collinspub.com

Audios
The "Business" Of Sewing
Marketing Your Sewing Business
Take The Fear Out Of Pricing
The "Business" Of Sewing Audio Album
Overcoming Doubt, Fear and Procrastination
*Overcoming Set
* means book included

Books
The "Business" Of Sewing Vol. 1
The "Business" Of Sewing Vol. 2
The "Business" Of Sewing (Original)
Marketing Your Sewing Business
Do You Sew For Profit: A Guide For
Wholesale, Retail and Consignment
Pricing Without Fear

Forms
Forms On Computer Disk
The Complete Set Of Forms
*Sew Pro Kit "A" (TBOS Original)
*Sew Pro Kit "B" (TBOS Original)
Home Décor/Interior Design
Marketing
Cornice Styles
TBOS = The "Business" Of Sewing

Index

A

Action Shots for Other Funds, 63
Afga's Color Guide, 33
Affiliate Networks, 99
Affiliate Programs, 98, 99
Aladdin software, 37
Announcing Your Business, 45
Answers to exercise, 82
Answers to questions, 120
Asian ad, 93
Asking for Funding, 64

B

Babies Make Good Business, 83
   Case Study, 86
Blending, 24
Borders, 30
Born to Shop, 79
Booth, Trade Show, 103
Brainstorm, 41
Brand Awareness, 19, 49 *See also* Consumer Motivation
Bridal, 75
Brochures, 35
Building a Strong Image, 19
Budget, 21, 26
   In terms of annual, monthly and quarterly expenditures, 26
   What to budget, 27
business cards, 10
Button, Jane Ambrose, 85

C

Calculate your CPM, 25
Call to Action, 24
Call Planning Worksheet, 51, 62
Calling Warm and Cold Leads, 58
Capture the reader's attention, 23
Catalogs, 35
Catering Your Promotional Material, 66
changing your portfolio, 40
Children's Clothing, 84-88
   fashion shows, 84
   keeping consistent look and feel, 85
CMYK, 32, 33 *See* Typesetting Guidelines
coding pieces, 105
comfortable environment, 50
company slogans, 21
competition's promotions, 26
Constant Contact, 100 *See also* Electronic Marketing
consumer demand, creating, 10, 15
Consumer Motivation, 47
convenience, 50
Cooperative Advertising, 27, 51
CorelDraw, 33 *See* Layout and Design
Coupons and Discounts, 48
Create communications, 10
Creating a sense of urgency, 23
Create an image, 20
Custom Tailoring, 79
Customer Contact Form, 51
customer profile, 16
Customer, who is mine, *See Who Is My Customer*

D

Dahl, Gary, 8
demographic data, 18
Designing Elements, 29, 95
Designing a Portfolio, 40
Designing a Website, 95
   Checklist for, 96
Designing Tips, 29
   Sample Site, 96
Desktop Publishing, 29

Determining Your Goal or Offer, 65
   catering your promotional material accordingly, 66
Determining Your Target Audience, 65
Developing a Logo, 20
Developing your list leads, 59
display your products, 35 *See* Brochures and Catalogs
Direct Mail, 65
   Direct Mail Marketing Checklist, 67
Dissect Form, 80
Distribution, 50
Do You Sew For Profit, 89

E

E-Commerce, 50
E-Mail Marketing Campaigns
Easy Upholstery, 90
Economy and Disposable Income, 49
Electronic Marketing, 100
encourage customers, 10
Entrepreneur, 47
Entry Points, 31
Established Relationships, 47
exchange client lists, 51
Exclusivity, 64
extended hours, 15

F

Finding Leads, 51
   how to, 51
First Impressions, 73
FlightCheck, 37
Flyers, 39
Font, 20
   font style, 31
   example, 31
   selection, 43
Free Marketing Cop-op Dollars, 63
Furniture stores, 89

G H

Giveaways, 27
using the library, 29
good slogan, 21
Grand Opening, 45
Graphics, 21, 34
Guide for Planning Your Advertising Timelines, 28
Guidelines for Designing Specific Ad Pieces, 43
Halftones, 32
Headings/Headlines, 30
   companion to, 31
Home Décor *See* Interior Design
   ad example, 94
   marketing for, 101

P

PageMaker, 33
Pantone, 33
Pet Rock, 7
Phone Call (The), 52 *See* Marketing Model
   tips for making the, 53
Photographs, 34
   effective use of, 35
Photoshop, 33
Planning and Execution, 64
   for Direct Mail, 65
potential customers, 14
potential for your products, 26
powerful headline, 23
Press Release, 99
Reliability of product and quality, 47
Repurposing, 10
RGB, 32

Index

I

Identifying Goods and Services, 13, 22
Identify the Audience, 26
Increase your Sales Volume, 26
(The) Informational, 24
initial attention, 15
Institutional or Service, 24
interact with your customers, 16
Interior Designers, 92
    ad example, 93

J K L

Kelly Paper Company, 34
Knowledge and Expertise, 47, 49
Layout and Design, 37
Lemon Kids Clothing, Case Study, 86-88
    ad, 87
Letterhead, 29, 43
Link Exchange, 99
List of Things To Do, 17

M

mail-order products, 16
Marketing, 7
    developing compelling material, 47
    objectives, 10
    strategy, 9
    electronic, 100
Marketing, Advertising, Promotions, 14, 18, 50
Market Analysis, 17
Marketing Campaign, 13 *See also* E-Mail Marketing Campaigns
    evaluation, 106
Marketing Ideas, 61
Marketing Model Description, 51
Marketing Model Outline, 56
Marketing To Travel Agents, 71
    how to find them, 72
    how to write a letter to them, 72
    telephoning them, 73
    meeting with them, 74
    thanking them, 75
matching goods and services, 14
Meeting, (The), 53 *See* Marketing Model
    tips for the, 54
Method of Payment, 48
monitoring your progress, 105
Most Effective Methods, for Generating Customer Leads, 59

N O

Newsletters, 39
    electronic, 100
Non-Traditional Marketing Methods, 60
Obsolescence, 49, *See* Consumer Motivation
Online Mailing, 67
Online Shopping Cart, 97
Opportunity to differentiate yourself, 23
    sample, 70
price, 48
Printing with color, 32
professional marketing consultant, 17
proofread, 43
Profile of My Customer, 79
Profiling Your Customer, 13
Promoting Your Business, 69
Promoting a new item or product, 24
Purchasing Decision, 9

Q R

Quality and Product Reliability, 47
Real Estate Sales, 92
Real Product and Service, 9
Recapturing your advertising dollars, 25

S

Sales Staff, 47
Sample Letter, 56, 57
Satisfy needs and wants, 15
Search Engines, 99
Seasons, 49
Service, 47
Shopping Cart, 97
Shopping the competition, 17
simple one-page flyer, 10
sizzle, 9, 23
Skyline, 102
Society and Peer Pressure, 49 *See* Consumer Motivation
specialty paper, 34
Spot Color, 33
store personnel, 18
store image and décor, 18
Strategy, 9
Study the competition, 17, 69
Study the clientele, 18
Stuffit Deluxe, Stuffit Expander, 37 *See* Layout and Design
Style, 48 *See* Consumer Motivation
subheadings, 30 *See also* Design Elements
subtle issues, 15
Summary, 41
Supply and Demand, 47

T U V

Target a specific audience, 24, 26
Target for free marketing money, 63
teasers, 35 *See* Brochures and Catalogs
Ten (10)-Foot Rule, 39 *See* Flyers
Textile Manufacturers, 92
tracking what sells, 106
Trade Shows, 101
    how to find them, 102
    booths, layout and design, 103
    preparing for, 103
Traditional Advertisements, 25
Travel Agents *See* Marketing to Travel Agents
Trends, 48
TrueMatch, 33
Trunk Shows, 62
Types of advertisement campaigns, 25
Types of payment methods, 18
Typesetting Guidelines, 32
    spacing, 32
    typesetting symbols, 32
    typeface, 32
    style, 32
United States Postal Service (USPS), 67
update your image, 19
Upholstery, 90
utilize contracts, 15
Virginia Quilting, 92

W X Y Z

Wants, Needs and Desires, 47
Web site, 10, 95-98 *See also* Designing a Website
What's in it for me?, 53
white space, 30
Who is my customer, 13
Why Custom Tailored Clothing, 80, 81
Why should you advertise, 23
Windows and Mac operating systems, 37
Window ad, 94
WinZip, 37 *See* Layout and Design
Word of Mouth, 48
Write a pitch letter, 63
Writing the Letter, 52, 54 *See* Marketing Model
    dissecting the letter, 54, 58
    letter template, 55
    sample letter, 56, 57

 **Marketing Your Sewing Business**   *$19.95*
How to Earn a Profit

Barbara Wright Sykes

A sewing business must be marketed in a special way to earn a profit. This book is designed for all types of sewing businesses and will show you how to: Get free publicity for a new and existing sewing business; make attractive Business Cards, Letterhead, Flyers, Brochures, and Catalogs complete with illustrations and examples. Get ideas for Logos, Graphics and Slogans. Develop a beautiful Website and Shopping Cart. Learn how to start and manage an e-mail marketing newsletter. Discover great ideas for marketing a sewing business using furniture stores, travel agents, day care centers, trunk shows, trade shows, home parties, the telephone and other innovative methods. Plus, how to get free advertising money for your sewing business and more! Order your copy today! $19.95   **ISBN: 0-9717824-3-1**

What's included...

The Power Of Marketing
Free Marketing Money
Getting Free Publicity
Writing a Press Release
Developing Image and Branding
Using Logos and Slogans
Selecting an Advertising Approach
Design Elements
Design: Business Cards, Letterhead,
Flyers Newsletters, Catalogs, Portfolios
Designing a Website and Brochure
Announcements and Grand Openings

Bridal and Special Occasion
Custom Tailoring—General Sewing
Baby and Children's Market
Home Décor—Interior Design
Creative Sewing and Crafts
Marketing Model
Direct Mail
Identify and Profile your Customer
Creating Demand & Attracting the Customer
Studying the Competition
Monitoring Your Progress
Shopping Carts—E-Commerce

Marketing Ideas for a Sewing Business:
- Mail Orders, Travel Agents
- Maternity Stores, Bowling Leagues
- Real Estate Offices, Furniture Stores
- TV/Movie Studios, Drama Depts.
- Day Care Centers, Cleaners
- Organizations and Associations
- Beauty Salons and Barber Shops
- Vendors and Affiliates
- Church, In-Kind Businesses
- Fashion, Trade and Trunk Shows

Barbara Wright Sykes
ISBN: 0-9632857-6-9   **Order Today!**

Pricing Without Fear $19.95

This book is a brilliantly sculpted step-by-step guide on pricing for profit—leaving no stone unturned. Barbara identifies obstacles associated with the fear of pricing, and is a master at helping you resolve them. As a bonus, Barbara's invited several of the industry's leading authorities to share their expertise. This book will help you replace doubt with the confidence in your ability to price for profit. *What's included...*

Pricing 101
Pricing Sheets
Pricing: Are You Afraid?
Pricing Effectively for Profit
Pricing: Consignment/Retail
Pricing: For The Bride
Pricing: For Show Dogs
Alterations—Making It Work!
Home Décor/Interior Design
Sewing For Children
How To Make A Profit
Work Efficiently
Developing Your Workspace

Pricing: Creative Sewing/Crafts
Pricing: Calculations
Pricing: Charts and Illustrations
Increase Your Profit Margin
Personal Pattern Line—Profit
Profit: Sell Other Products
Turn Scraps Into Cash
Studio Expansion
Business tools
Fabric/Notions: Wholesale
Overhead: Saving Money
Is It Time For A Raise?
Money—Getting Bank Loans

Coming Soon *Pricing Without Fear* gets a New Cover!

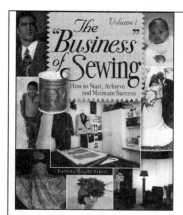

Barbara Wright Sykes

ISBN: 0-9717824-1-5

NEW

The "Business" Of Sewing: Volume 1 $19.95

Industry Price Lists
Top 20 States for Sewers
The Sewing Industry
Myth about Sewing Pros
Right Attitude for Business
Skills Inventory
Visualization Exercise
Specialist vs. Generalist
Tackling your Fears
How to avoid Frustration
Working for Yourself
Tragedy into Triumph
Professional Presence
Client Relationships
Conducting Interviews
Fitting and Pickup
Delivery Appointments
Installation Appointments

Getting the Capital
Where to go for Help
Special Loan Programs
Funding Requirements
Cash Flow Projections
Inventory & Marketing Plan
Goals. Mission statement
Setting standards
Business and Financial Plan
Sewing Security: Insurance
Location and Equipment
License, Permits and Zoning
Design: Office and Studio
How to Hire a Contract
Human Resources
Buying in Bulk and Co-op
Supplies, Finding Suppliers
Sample Supplier Letter

How to Request Payment
Types of Payment Methods
Getting a Merchant Account
Credit Card Processing
Collecting Money
Bounced Checks
2 Sample letters
3 Sample Collection Letters
Business Policy
Mentors and Networking
Sewing Forum
Continuing Education
Online classes
Sewing Solo vs. a Partner
Sewing as a Corporation
Sewing Software
Easy Business Forms
Sewing Machine Update

Barbara Wright Sykes

ISBN: 0-9717824-2-3

NEW

The "Business" Of Sewing: Volume 2 $19.95

Pricing For Profit
Handling Price Resistance
Your Price List
Sample Price List
Pricing Methods & Formulas
Pricing Exercises
Handling Murphy's Law
Effective Time Management
Scheduling Projects
Delegating Sewing Task
Keeping Good Books
Business Activities
Computerized Accounting
Shopping Carts & Gateways
Websites and Domain Names
Online Merchant Accounts
Benefiting from Technology
Software and Computers
Learning Software Easier

Understanding Production
Production Time Analysis
Project Inventory List
How to Make a Price List
Putting it all together
Using a Price List
Testing your Knowledge
Pricing Exercise
Labor Calculations
Contract Charges
Production Reviews
Marketing Strategy
Identifying Your Market
Profiling Your Customer
Studying Your Competition
Designing a Line
Planning a Line
Pricing the Line
Consumer Price Lists

Home Décor Yardage Chart
Attracting Clients
Cost Effective Marketing
Advertising and Promotions
Diversification
Changing your Pricing
Goods and Services
Home vs. Commercial
Employees &Subcontractors
Employment Application
Independent Contractors
Fabricators
Mail-Order Business
Teaching: Fees and Forms
Developing Contracts
Conducting Seminars
Writing Articles & Books
Types of Publishing
Profiting: Audios & Videos

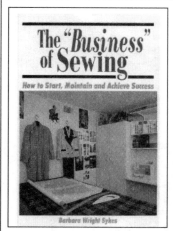

Barbara Wright Sykes
ISBN: 0-9632857-5-0

The "Business" Of Sewing: Original $19.95

This is the very first book where Barbara Wright Sykes gives you a candid look into how she earned $800 to $1,000 a day in an incredibly profitable sewing business. The book has sold over 150,000 copies, ranking it the #1 leader in the field of sewing for profit! *The "Business" Of Sewing* received Amazon.com customers highest honor—a Five-Star rating!

It received rave reviews from: *Nancy Zieman, Sew News, McCall's and Simplicity Pattern Companies*. If you desire to learn how a successful entrepreneur got started sewing for profit, this book is for you. We are proud to offer Barbara's original book, *The "Business" Of Sewing*.

The book also comes packaged in the following: The Sew Pro Kit "A" and Sew Pro Kit "B", which includes 23 business forms for those who sew for profit. This book will be your constant reference!

Getting Started
Choosing a Business
Time Study
Business Plan, Setting Goals
Taxes, License, Permits
Record Keeping
Where to Sell – What to Sell
Finding Clients

Looking Professional
Business Cards & Press Releases
Advertising
Reflect the Proper Images (Sales)
Designing Your Work Area
Displays

Pricing and Production
Buying Wholesale
Buying Supplies
Wholesale vs. Retail
Working Efficiently
Using Scraps
Pricing (Service/Product)

Promotion
Follow-up & Mailing Lists
Dealing with Clients
Problem Solving
Networking
Expectations
Resources

Home Décor—Interior Design Forms – More than 70 Forms

Order Now!

70 plus skillfully designed forms for sewing pros operating workrooms and for those who contract out labor. There are forms for conducting business in a commercial location as well as operating from your home. As an added bonus we have included forms with graphics. The forms included the following:

- Business, Record keeping, Advertising
- Sample: Formulas and Calculations
- Work Orders and Worksheets
- Bedcovers, Bed skirts
- Canopy, Pillows, Shams
- Drapery, Valances, Top Treatments
- Cascades, Shades, Swags
- Plus much more.

- Cornice, Pelmets, Lambrequin
- Tables Cloths, Skirts and Toppers
- Placemats, Napkins
- Upholstery: Sofa, Chairs
- Headboards, Folding Screens
- Embroidery and Quilting
- Floor and Wall Coverings
- Some forms have graphics!

How To Purchase Forms: **CD Disk** ♦ $49.00 **Paper Forms** ♦ $55.00
CD Formats: Word, Excel, PDF-MAC   **70+ Forms** ♦**Graphics**

The Complete Set Of Forms $30.00

Need Forms? We've Done All The Work For You! You don't have to start from scratch. The packet includes forms to help you sewing for profit. Included are: *Contracts* for consultation and production; *The Project Worksheet* to calculate actual labor cost for projects; the *Request Form* to control client appointments and screen potential clients while educating them on your business with the *Client Call Sheet*. Avoid price resistance with the use of the *Business Policy*. Insure accuracy of all measurements with the *Measurement Chart*. Avoid mistakes on projects with the *Pattern Adjustment Check List*. Assess your actual production time and increase your profit with three of the most important forms: the *Project and Task List, Time and Motion Chart*, and the *Price List Worksheet*. Desire to teach, we have all the forms. Expand your business with these two forms: *Independent Contractors Agreement* or the *Employment Application*. Want to price for consignment or put items into retail establishments—we have it all. There are "**23**" Business Forms.

Forms On Computer Disk $35.99   "23" Forms Included

The forms above are also available on computer disk for your convenience! Including contracts, price sheets, measurement charts, and more. Everything you need to achieve success as a sewing professional is available on computer disk for customization.
PC and PDF for MAC

Product List

See Shipping and Handling Fees on Order Form page 119

TITLE	PRICE	Qty.	TOTAL
Book: Overcoming Doubt, Fear & Procrastination ISBN: 0-9632857-7-7	$24.95		
Workbook: Overcoming Doubt, Fear & Procrastination ISBN: 0-9632857-8-5	$9.95		
Audio: Overcoming Doubt, Fear & Procrastination ISBN: 0-9632857-9-3	$16.95		
Set: Overcoming Set – Includes all 3 -- Book, Workbook and Audio	$46.85		
Book: Pricing Without Fear ISBN: 0-9632857-6-9	$19.95		
Book: The "Business" of Sewing: Volume 1 ISBN: 0-9717824-1-5 **"NEW"**	$19.95		
Book: The "Business" of Sewing : Volume 2 ISBN: 0-9717824-2-3 **"NEW"**	$19.95		
Book: The "Business" of Sewing (Original) ISBN: 0-9632857-5-0	$19.95		
Book: Do You Sew For Profit: A Guide For Wholesale, Retail and Consignment ISBN: 0-9717824-0-7 **"NEW"**	$19.95		
Book: Marketing Your Sewing Business: How To Earn A Profit ISBN: 0-9717824-3-1 **"NEW"**	$19.95		
Kit: Sew Pro Kit "A" – Includes: The "Business" Of Sewing – Original and The Complete Set Of Forms **"NEW"**	$40.00		
Kit: Sew Pro Kit "B" – Includes: The "Business" Of Sewing – Original and Forms On Computer Disc **"NEW"**	$45.00		
Audio Tape 1. The "Business" of Sewing	$16.95		
Audio Tape 2. Taking The Fear Out Of Pricing	$16.95		
Audio Tape 3. Marketing Your Sewing Business	$16.95		
Audio Album The "Business" of Sewing ISBN: 0-9632857-1-8	$45.00		
Forms: Complete Set of Forms	$30.00		
Forms: Forms on Computer Disk	$35.99		
Forms: Home Décor - Interior Design Forms CD Format for MAC and PC **"NEW"**	$49.00		
Forms: Home Décor - Interior Design Forms Paper Forms **"NEW"**	$55.00		
Forms: Marketing Forms Paper Forms **"NEW"**	$25.00		
Forms : Marketing Forms CD Format for MAC and PC **"NEW"**	$20.00		
Forms : Cornice Styles Paper Forms **"NEW"**	$ 1.00		
Forms : Cornice Styles CD Format for MAC and PC **"NEW"**	$ 5.00		
Newsletter: Back Issues of The "Business" of Sewing Newsletter –all "8" **Special-Includes Pricing Issue!**	$17.00		
Book: Creative Sewing As A Business **"NEW"**	$19.95		
Book: Fashion For Profit **"NEW"**	$45.00		
Video: Windows 101 **"NEW"**	$20.00		
Video: The Perfect Pillow **"NEW"**	$20.00		
Video: Pillow Parade **"NEW"**	$20.00		
Video: Sensational Swags & Jabots **"NEW"**	$20.00		
Video: Straw Hat Class **"NEW"**	$39.95		
See Shipping and Handling Fees on Order Form on page 119			
You may use this form to select the items you want then fill in the order form			
Prices subject to change without notice.			
1-800-795-8999 or www.collinspub.com			
See a comprehensive selection of product on our website.			

COLLINS PUBLICATIONS Since 1991
We thank you for your interest in our company. We look forward to serving you. Please let us know if you received your order in a prompt and timely manner. Our goal is to bring you maximum satisfaction. If you have any concerns please do not hesitate to call me personally: **909-590-2471**.
Thank You,

Ann Collins

Join Barbara Wright Sykes for one of her "Powerful Seminars"

Please Print all information
Check all seminars you would like to attend listed below

Name: _____

Address-City-Zip _____

_____

_____

Hm Phone _____ Wk Phone _____

Business _____

Fax _____ Email _____

How many in your party? _____ Will you need a hotel? ☐Yes ☐No

Which do you prefer: ☐ Weekend ☐ Weekday

List 3 dated you prefer: Example: 1. May 19

1. _____ 2. _____ 3. _____

Mail to: Collins Publications 3233 Grand Ave. Suite N-294C
Chino Hills, CA 91709 • 909-590-2471 • Fax: 909-628-9330

It's an experience you won't forget! We're scheduling ten in California. If you would like to attend send in this form. List the month and dates desired.

Meeting Planners: To book Barbara for your next seminar or workshop call and ask for Ann at: 909-590-2471

Barbara Wright Sykes

Author
Speaker
Trainer
Consultant

To book Barbara Call:
909-590-2471

$1.00

Catalog - Color

Seminar Topics

☐ **Overcoming Doubt, Fear and Procrastination**
☐ **The "Business" Of Sewing**
☐ **Marketing Your Sewing Business**

☐ **Getting Published**
☐ **Pricing Without Fear**
☐ **Retail, Wholesale and Consignment**

ORDER FORM

COLLINS PUBLICATIONS
3233 Grand Ave., Suite N-294C
Chino Hills, CA 91709
Website: www.collinspub.com

Credit Card Orders: (800) 795-8999
Fax Orders: (909) 628-9330
Customer service: (909) 590-2471
Email Orders: collins@collinspub.com

☐ Regular Shipping
☐ Airmail Shipping
☐ Next Day Air

TITLE	PRICE	QTY.	TOTAL
COLOR CATALOG	1.00		
Free Black/White Flyer			
Attach a separate sheet for additional products. Bring totals forward. Prices subject to change without notice		Subtotal	
How did you hear about us?		Minus Coupon	
		New Sub-Total	
Use appropriate state tax		Tax (8% CA Residents)	
Check type of shipping above: Regular Shipping Takes 3-5 weeks; Airmail takes 3-5 working days		Shipping & Handling	
Name	Date	Total (US Funds Only)	
Company	Work Phone	Fax	
Home Phone	E-Mail	Website	
Address			
City	State	ZIP	
☐ Cash ☐ Check # ☐ Money Order ☐ MasterCard ☐ Visa ☐ Discover ☐ American Express			
Credit Card #		Exp. Date	
Name on Card	Signature		

Regular US		Air Mail US		Next Day US		Canada		International	
$1.01 to $15	$5.00	$1.01 to $15	$7.00	$1.01 to $15	$17.15	$1.01 to $15	$8.05	$1.01 to $15	$10.05
$16 to $25	$5.95	$16 to $25	$8.00	$16 to $25	$20.15	$16 to $25	$9.05	$16 to $25	$12.05
$26 to $50	$7.95	$26 to $50	$10.00	$26 to $50	$26.15	$26 to $50	$11.05	$26 to $50	$14.05
$51 to $100	$9.95	$51 to $100	$12.00	$51 to $100	$32.15	$51 to $100	$13.05	$51 to $100	$16.05
$101 to $150	$10.95	$101 to $150	$14.00	$101 to $150	$38.15	$101 to $150	$15.05	$101 to $150	$18.05
$151 to $175	$12.95	$151 to $175	$16.00	$151 to $175	$43.15	$151 to $175	$17.05	$151 to $175	$20.05

Shipping Rates
Regular Takes 3-5 weeks
Air Mail is only 3-5 work days
Call for additional rates.

Slogan Answers

Slogan	Company or Product
You deserve a break today	McDonalds
Be all that you can be	U.S. Army
M'm, M'm good	Campbell's 1930s
Double your pleasure, double your fun	Wrigley's Doublemint Gum
It's the Real Thing	Coca Cola 1970
A little dab'll do ya	Brylcreem
Diamonds are forever	DeBeers
Just do it	Nike
The pause that refreshes	Coca-Cola 1929
Tastes great, less filling	Miller Lite
Good to the last drop	Maxwell House
Breakfast of champions	Wheaties 1930s
Does she ... or doesn't she?	Clairol
Only her hairdresser knows for sure	Clairol
When it rains it pours	Morton Salt 1912
Where's the beef?	Wendy's
The Uncola. Never had it; never will	7 UP 1970s
99 and 44/100% Pure	Ivory Soap 1882
Snap! Crackle! and Pop	Kellogg's Rice Krispies 1940s
Look, Ma! No cavities	Crest toothpaste 1958
Melts in your mouth, not in your hands	M&Ms 1954
Takes a licking and keeps on ticking	Timex 1950s.
Have it your way	Burger King 1973
Only you can prevent forest fires	Smokey the Bear U.S. Forest Service
Look sharp, feel sharp	Gillette 1940s
You'll wonder where the yellow went	Pepsodent 1956
Ring around the collar	Wisk detergent 1968
When you care enough to send the very best	Hallmark 1930s
501 Blues	Levi's jeans 1984
From the Land of Sky Blue Waters	Hamm's beer 1950s
Reach out and touch someone	AT&T 1979
We'll leave a light on for you	Motel 6 1988
Plop plop, fizz, fizz	Alka-Seltzer
Because you're worth it	L'Oreal
Bet you can't eat just one	Lay's potato chips
Sometimes I feel like a nut, sometimes I don't	Almond Joy
What smells fresh, stays fresh	Gain
The cross your heart bra	Playtex
Tell a friend	Alpha beta
A hint of minty freshness	Scope
Poppin' fresh dough boy	Pillsbury
It's very good chocolate	Boscoe